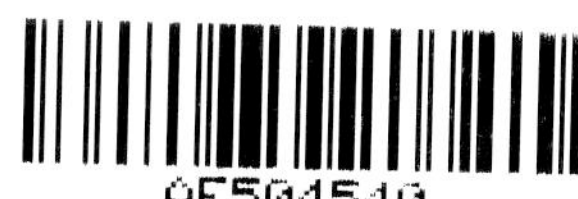
AF504540

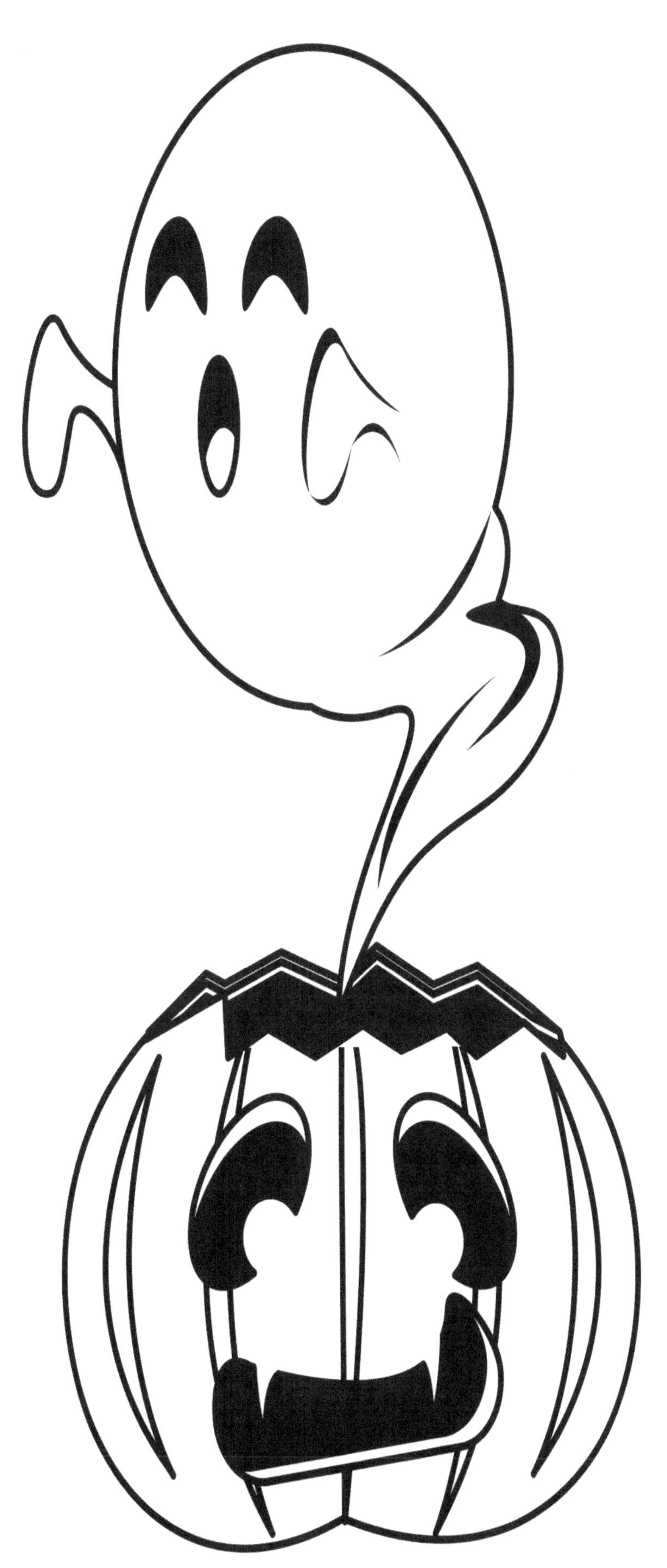

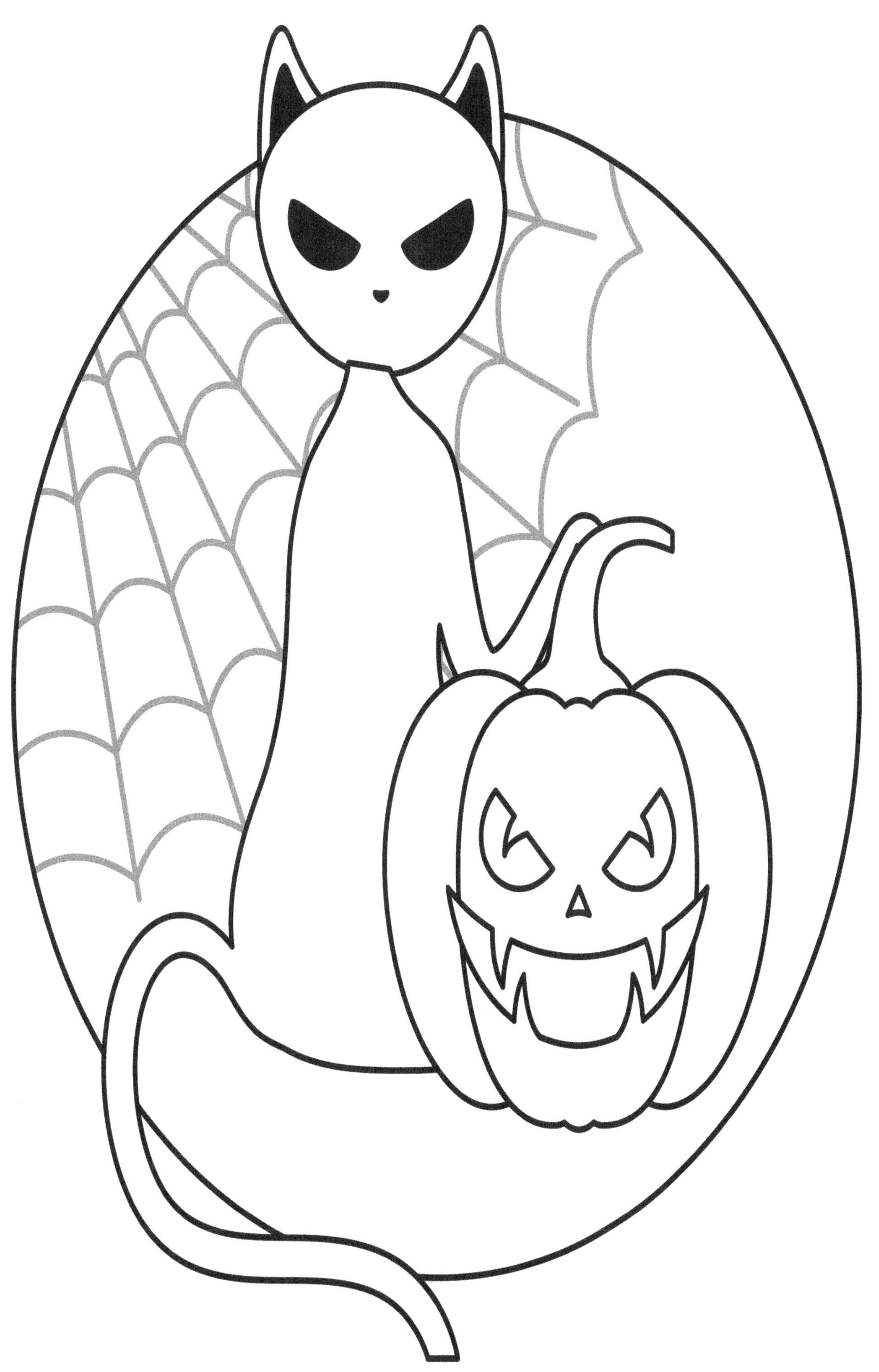

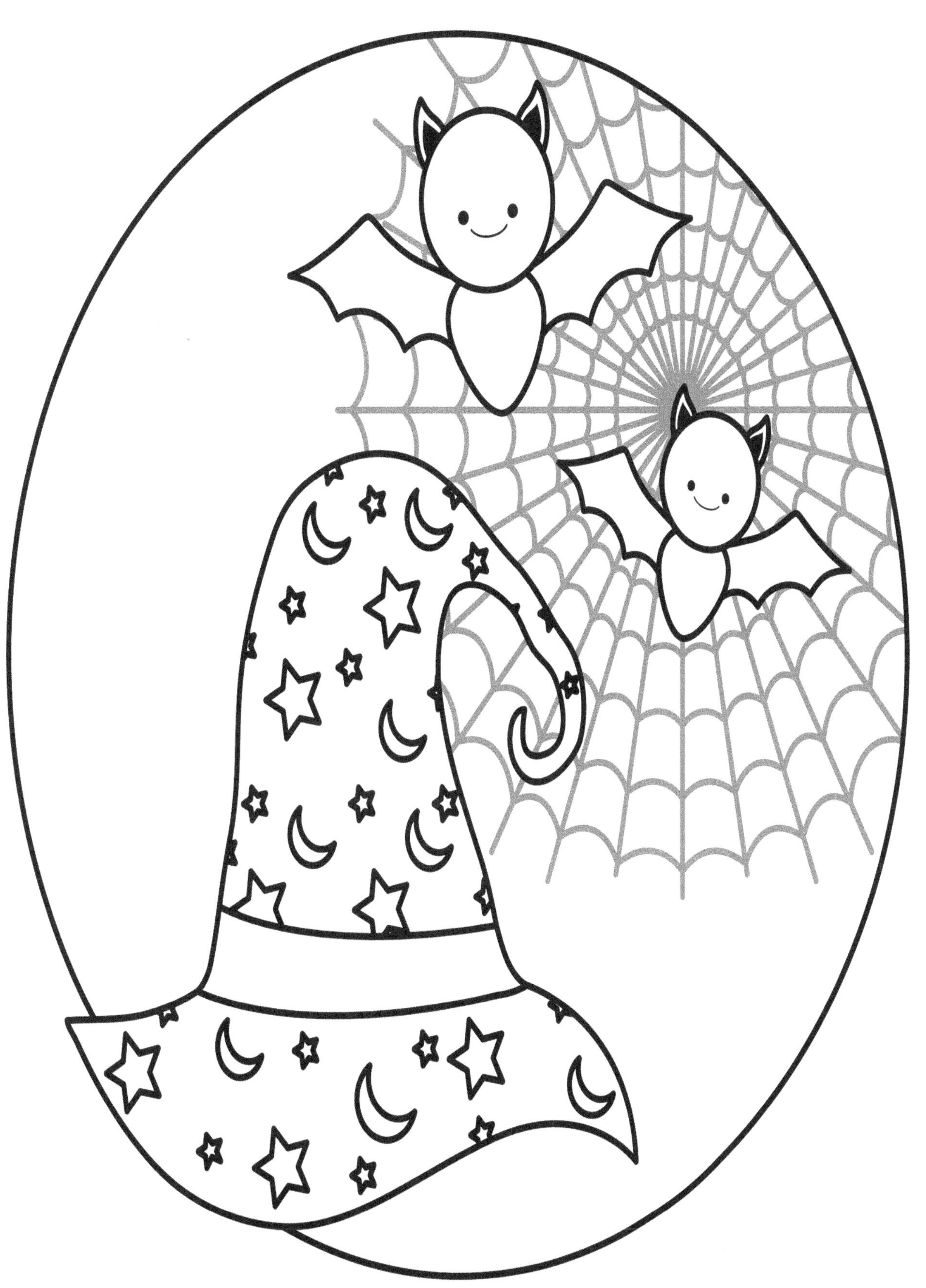

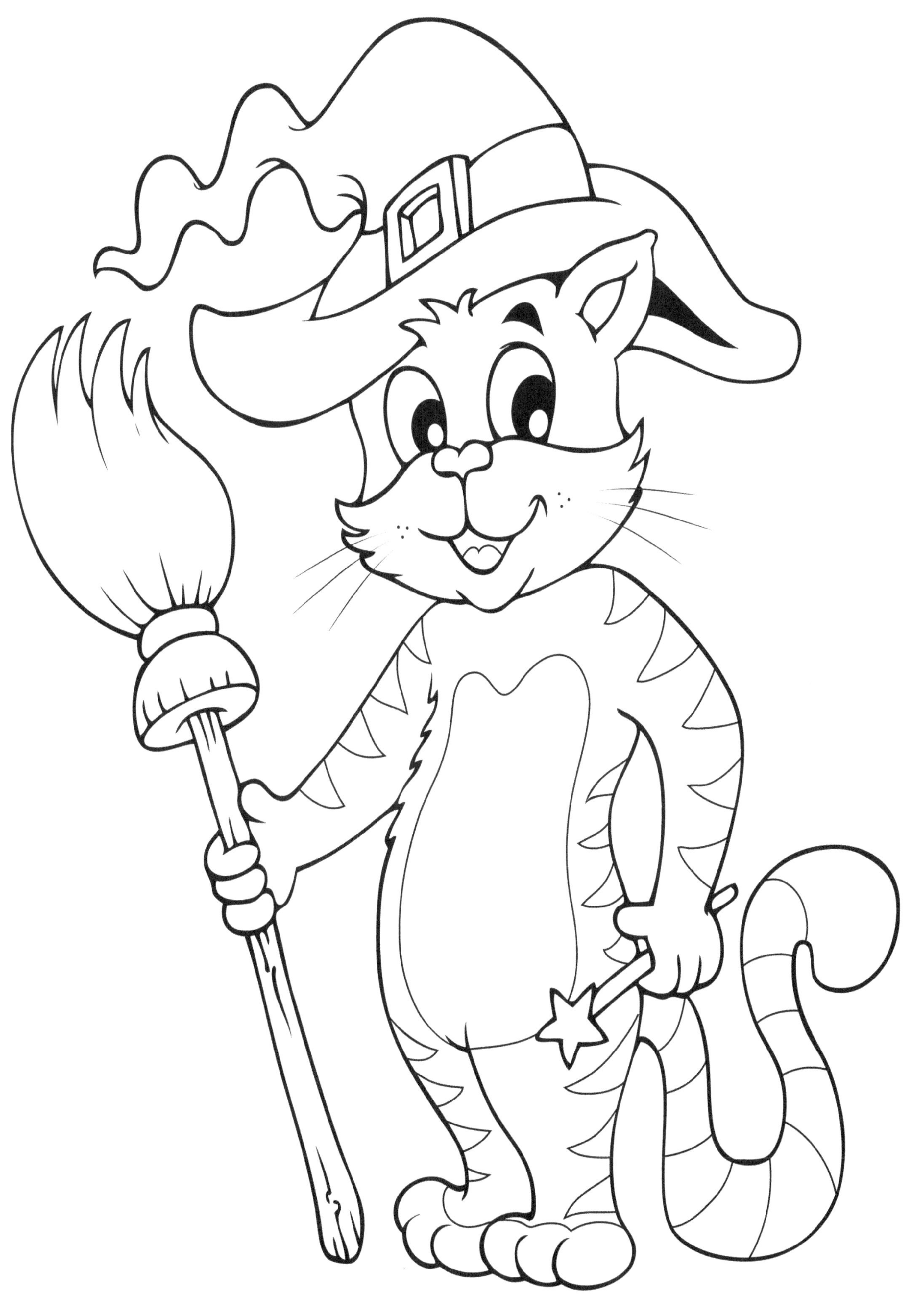

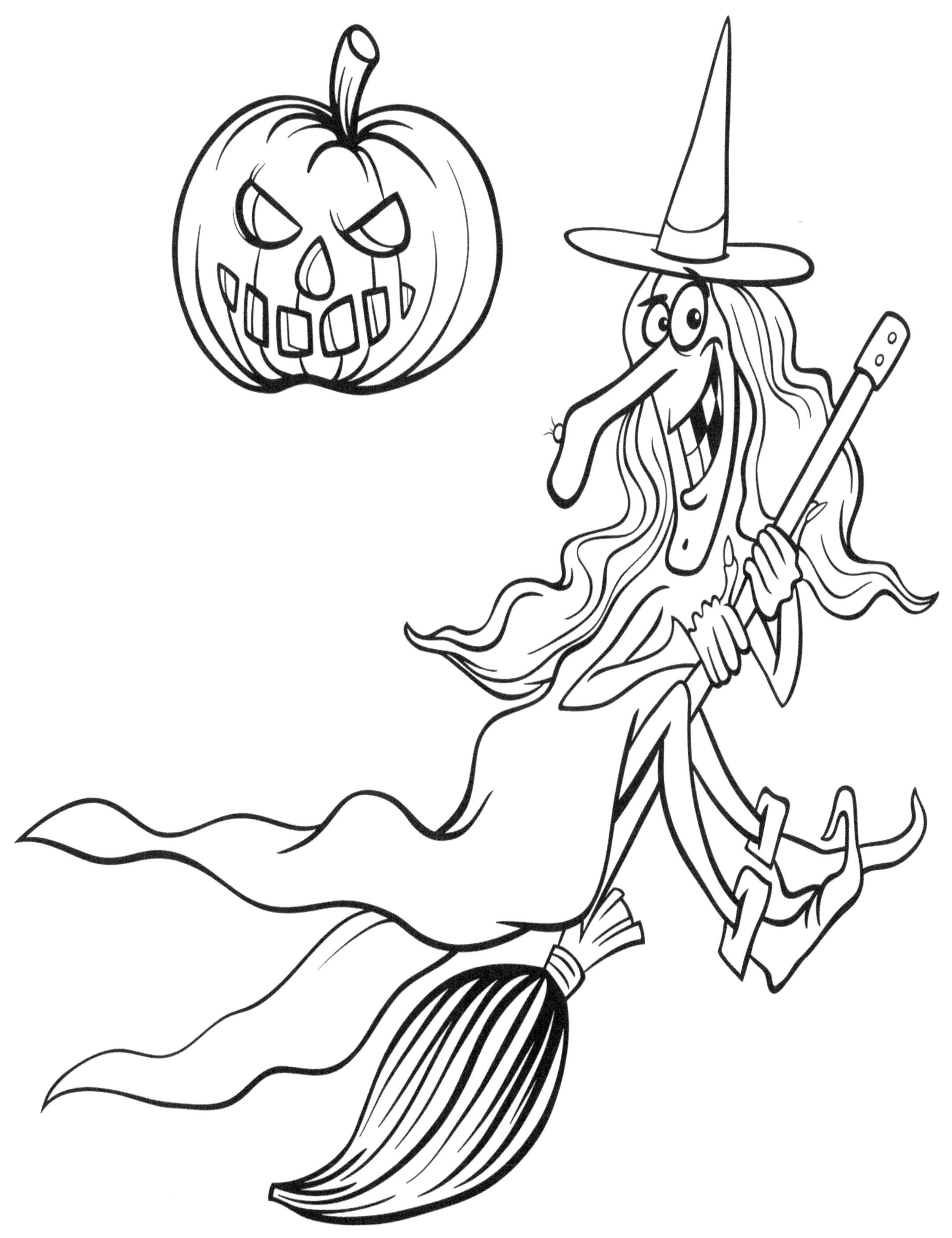

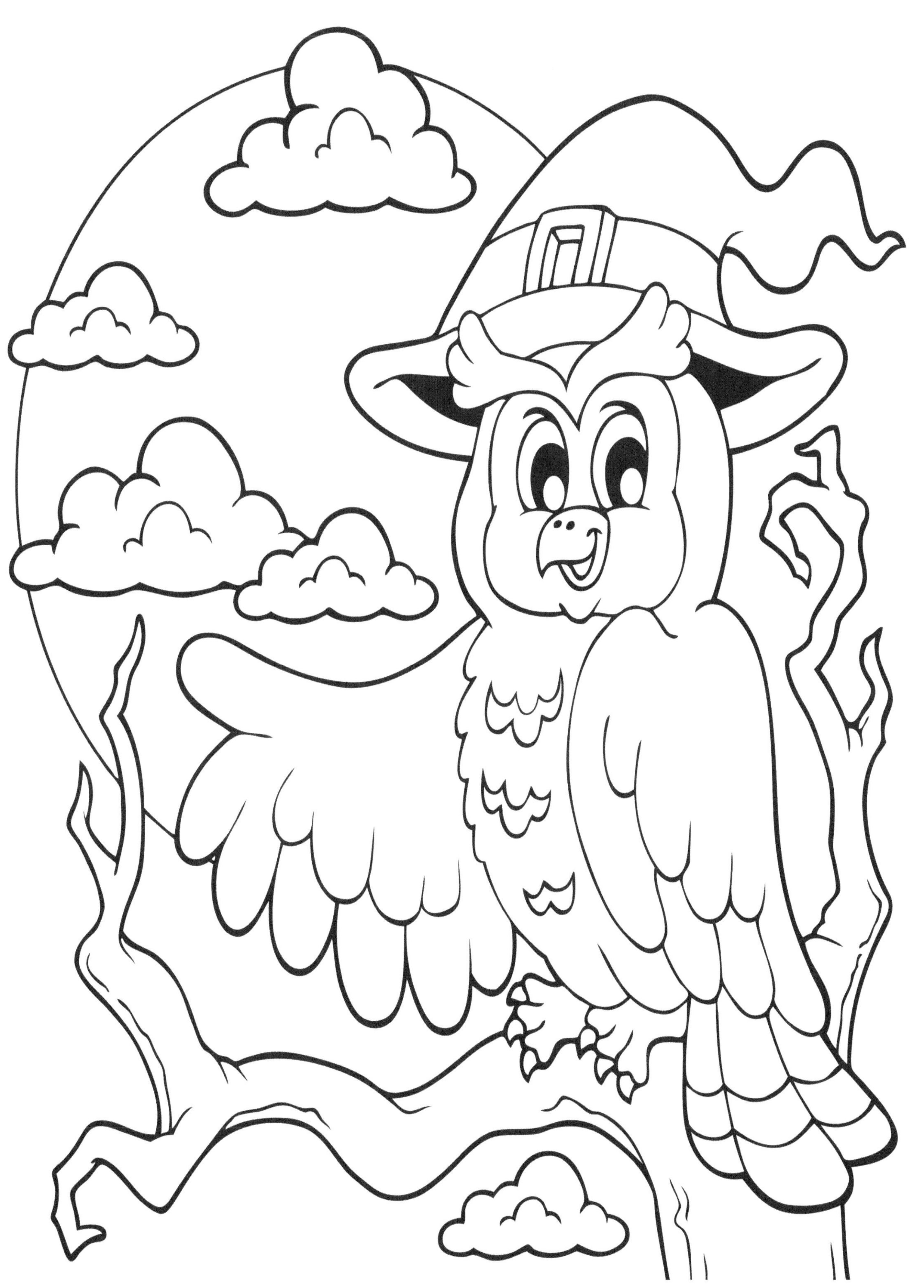

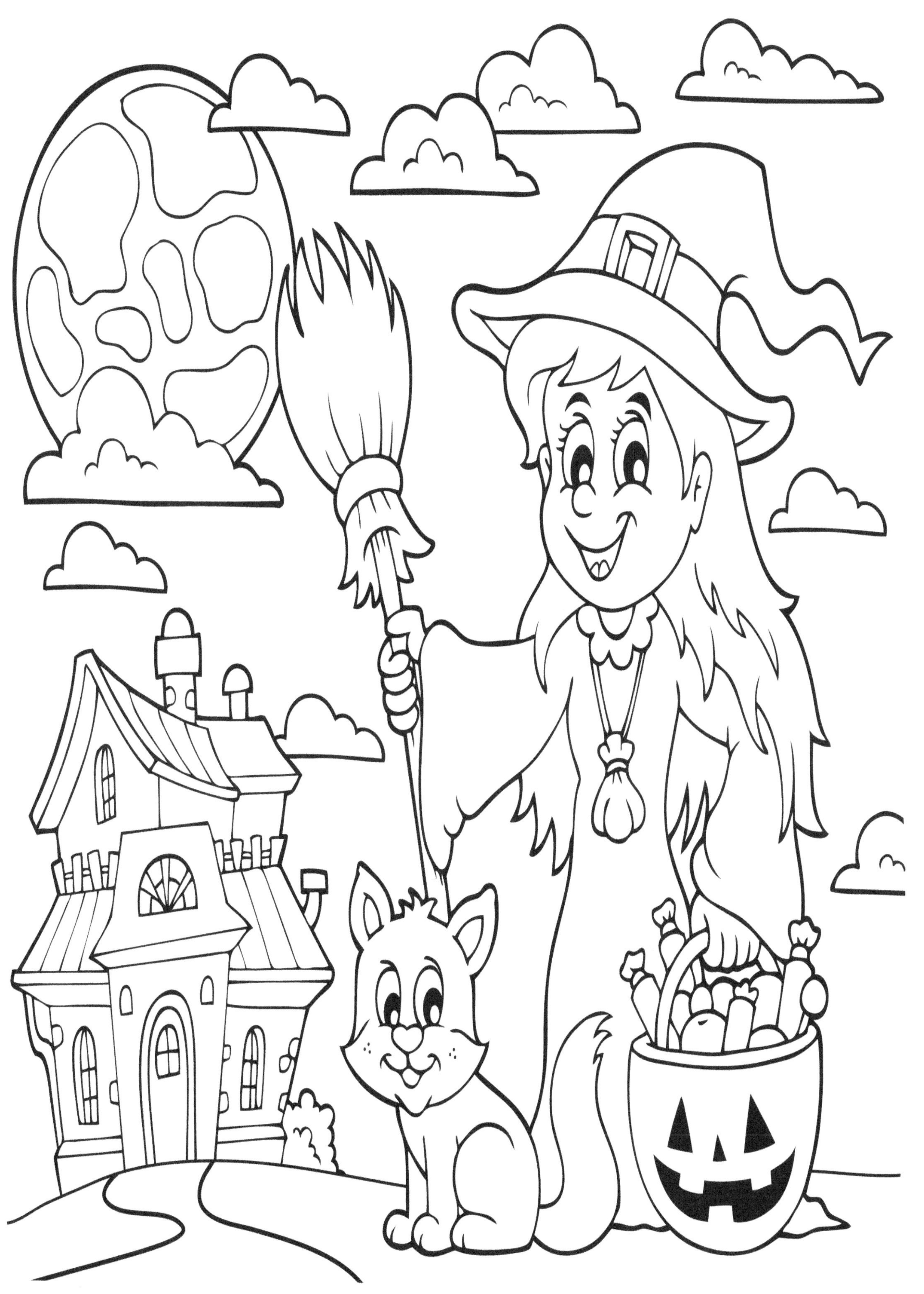

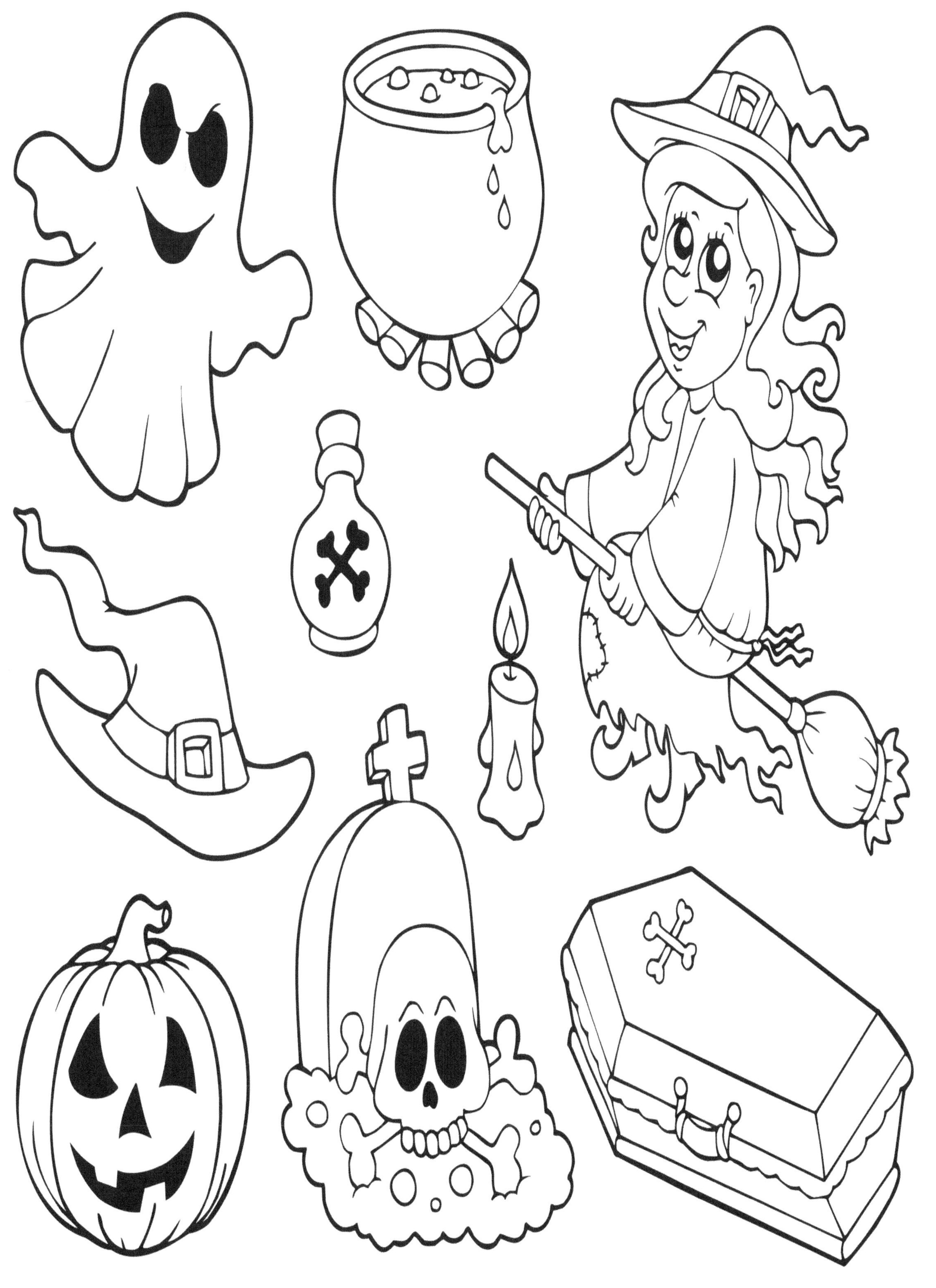

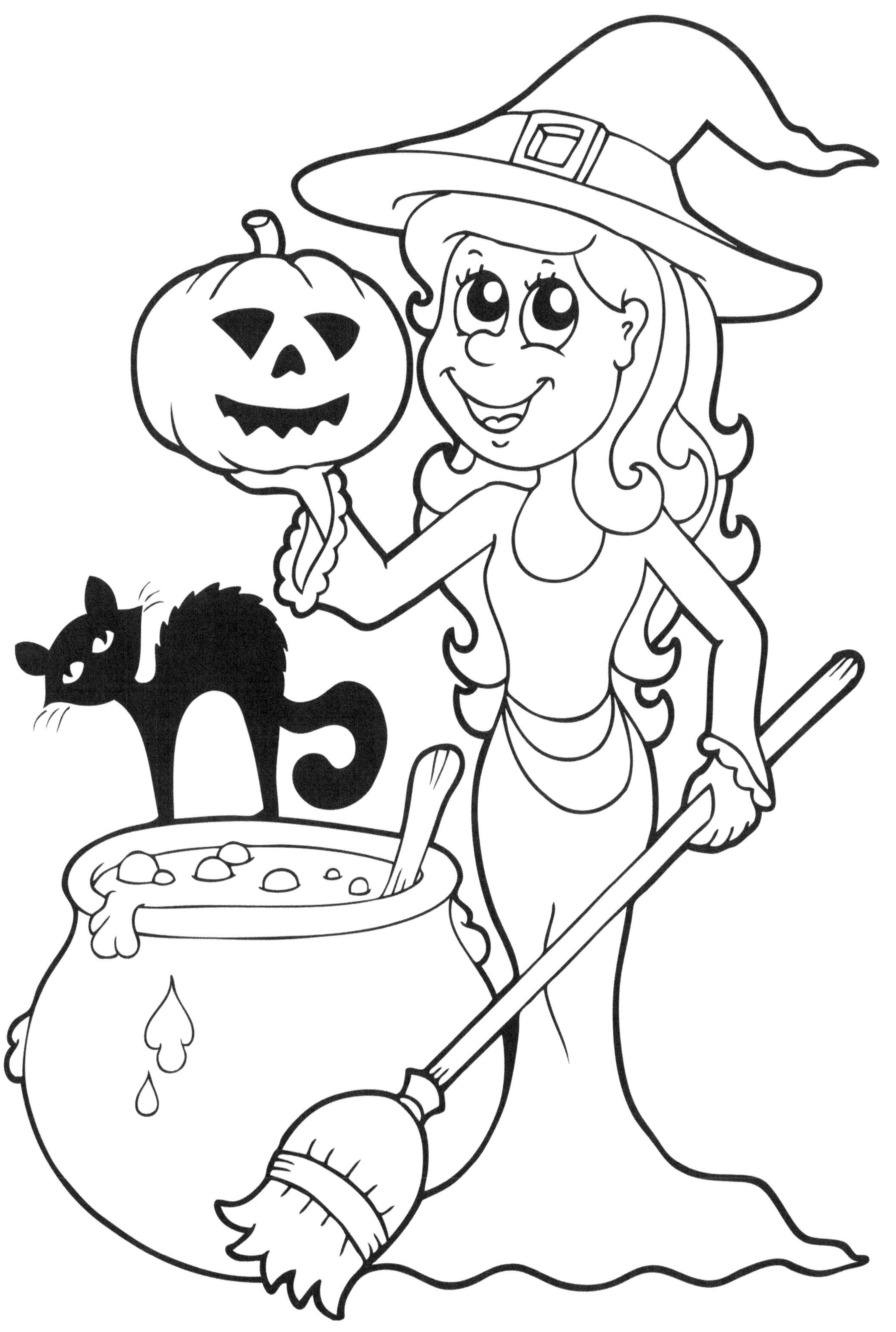

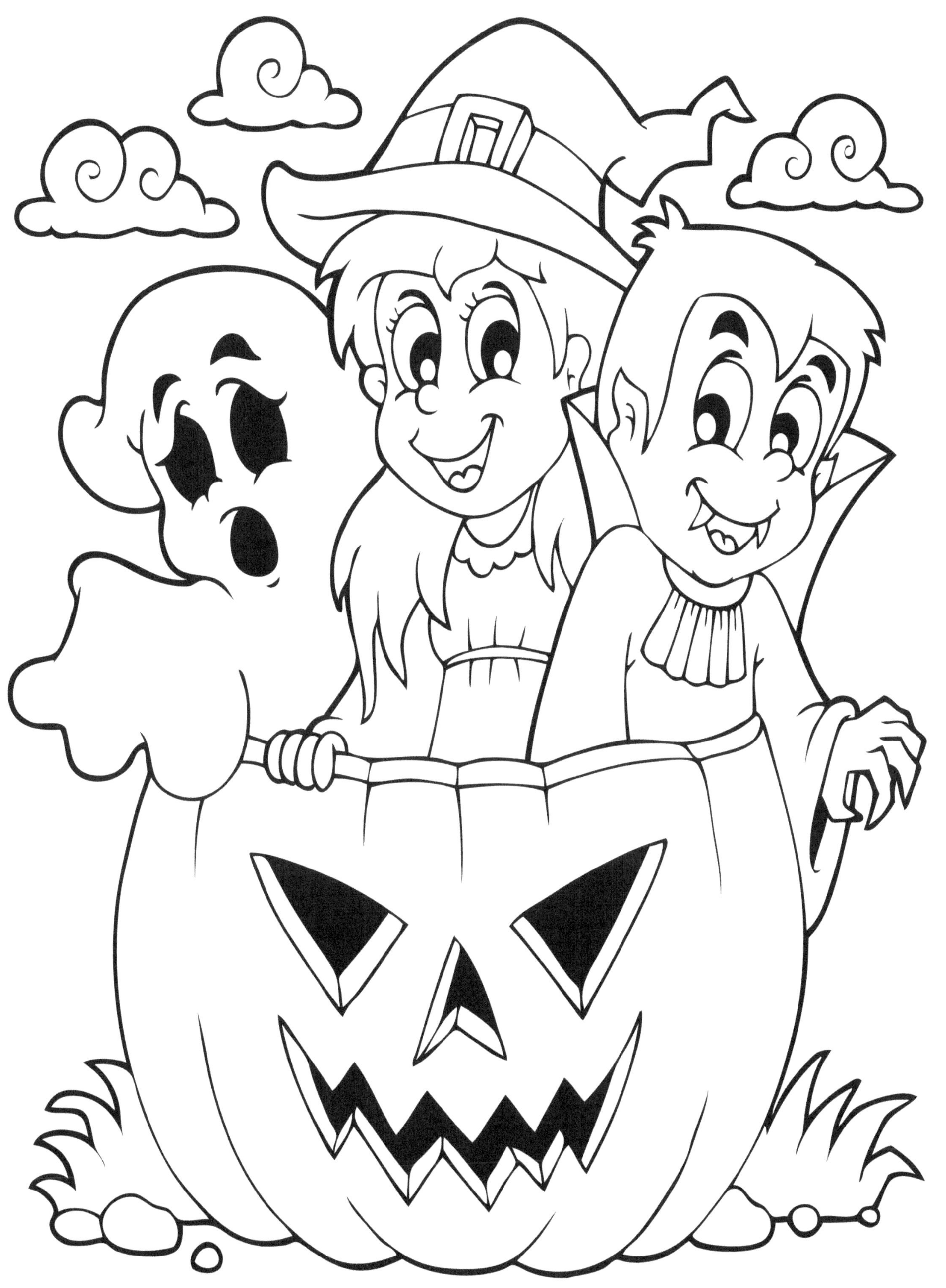

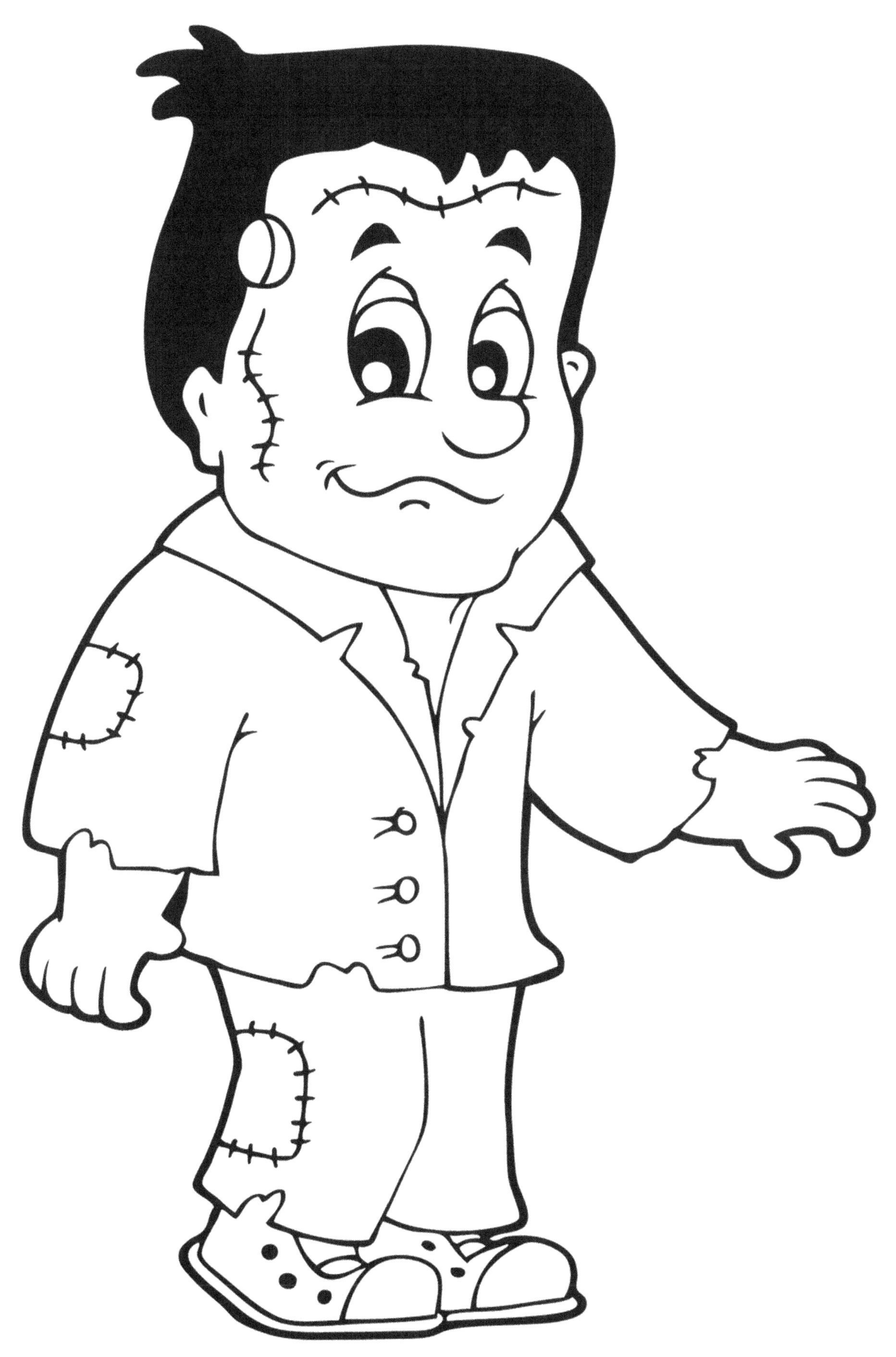

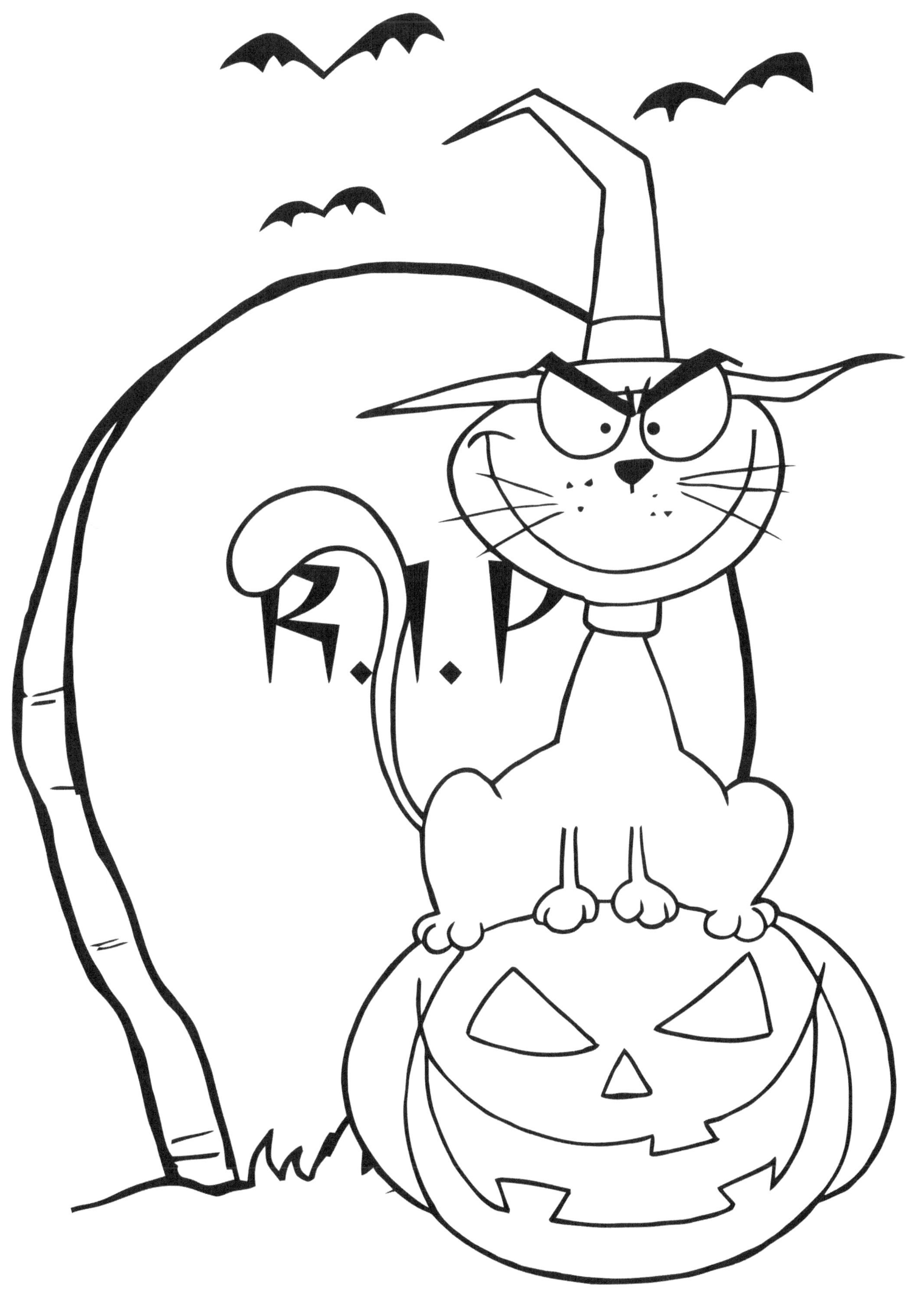

R.I.P

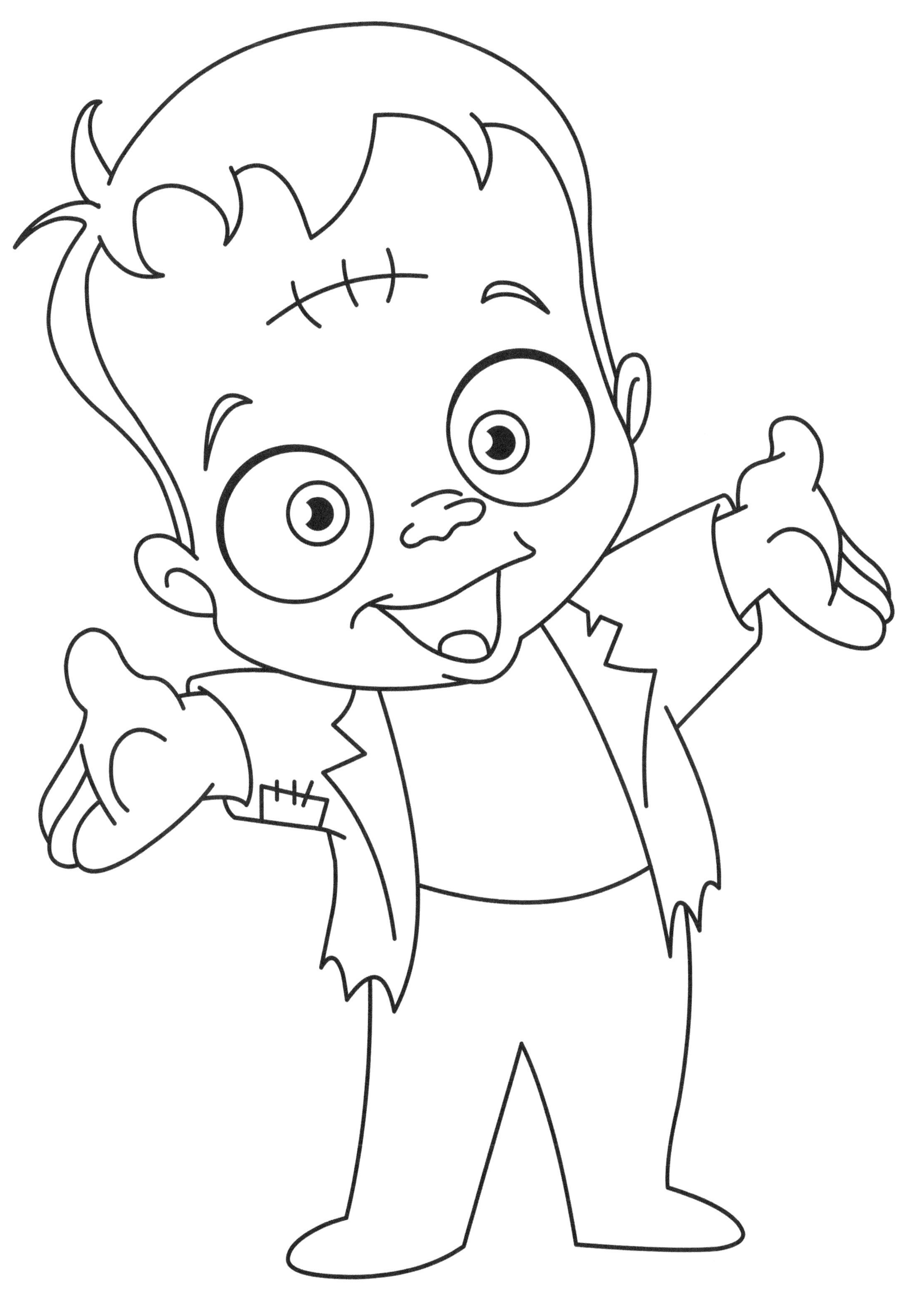

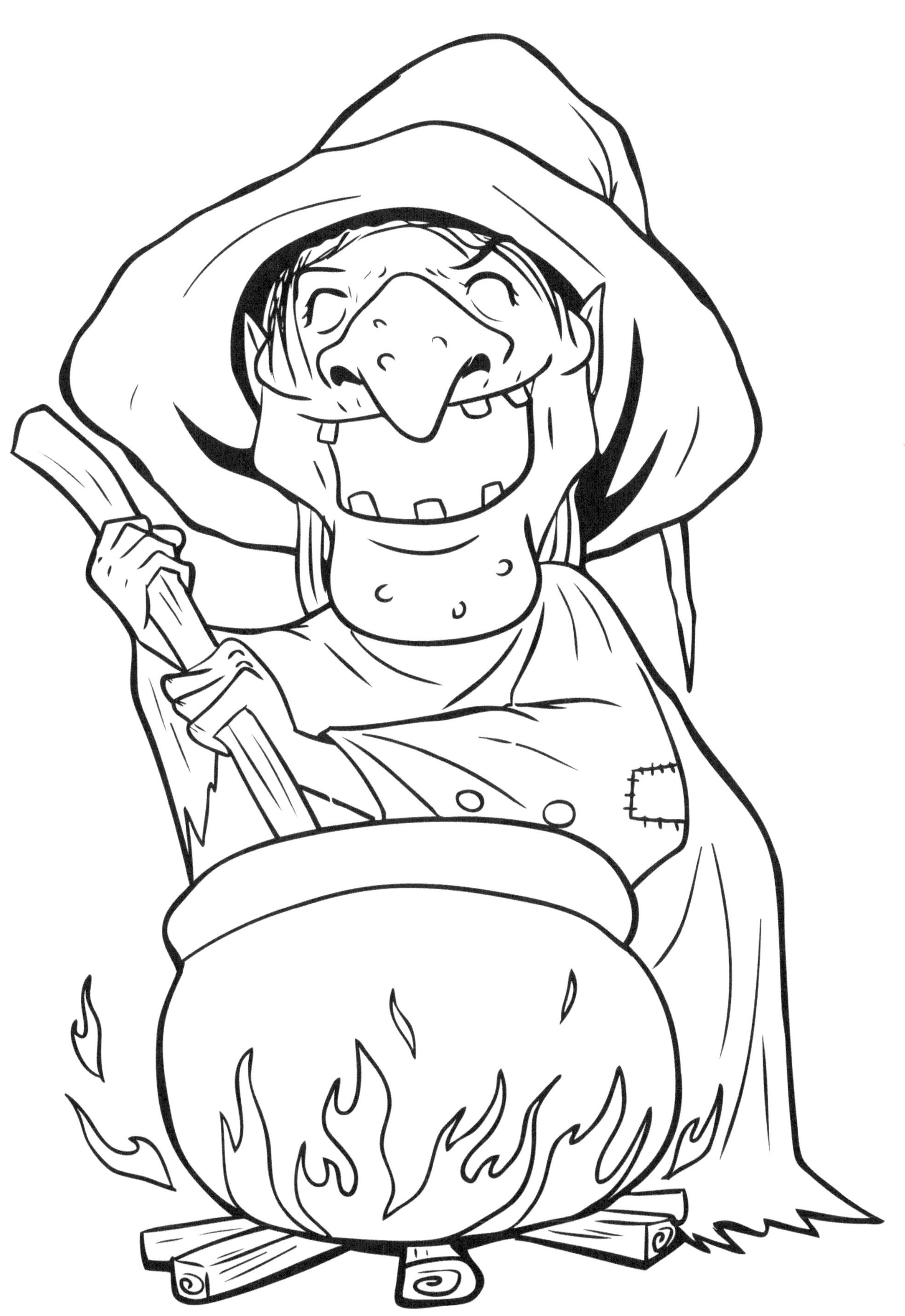

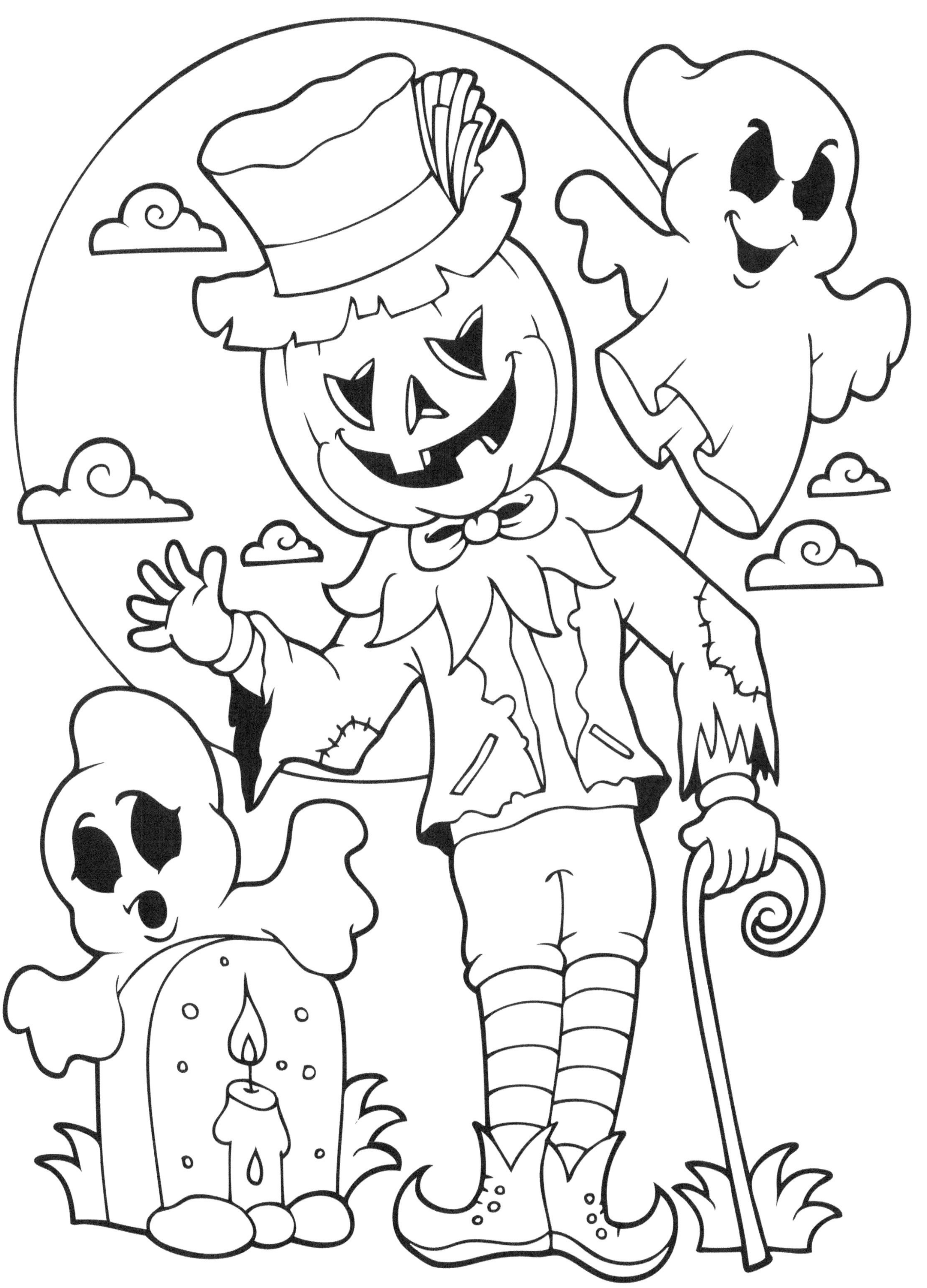

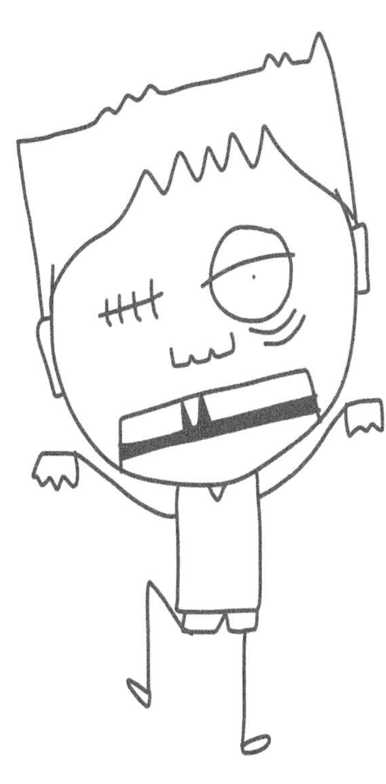
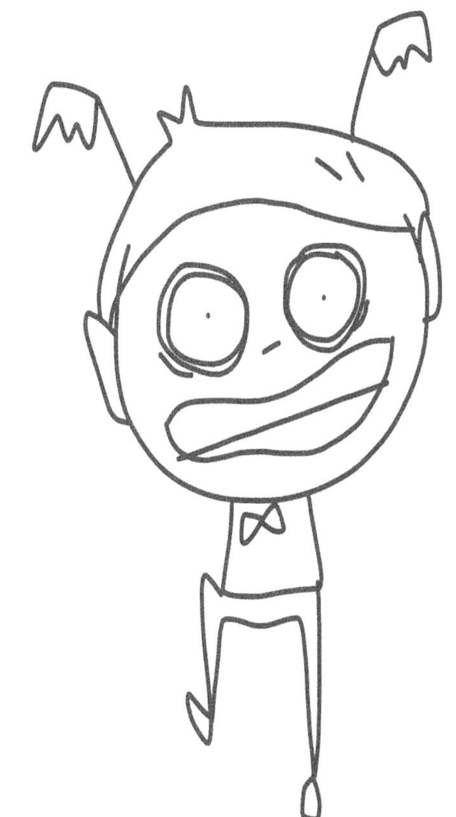
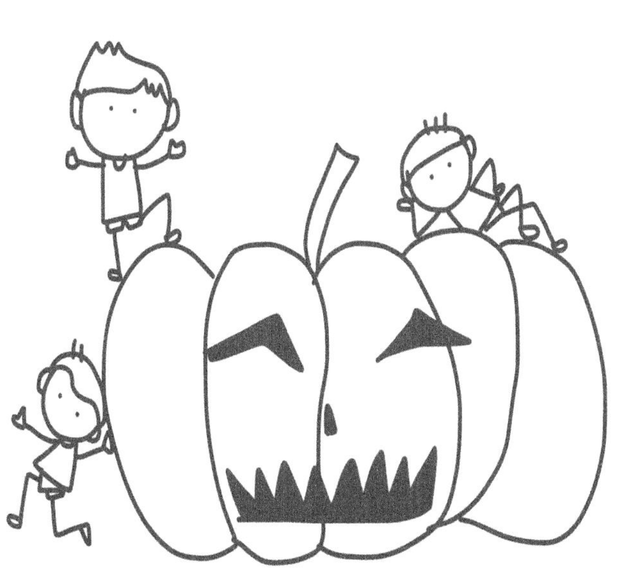
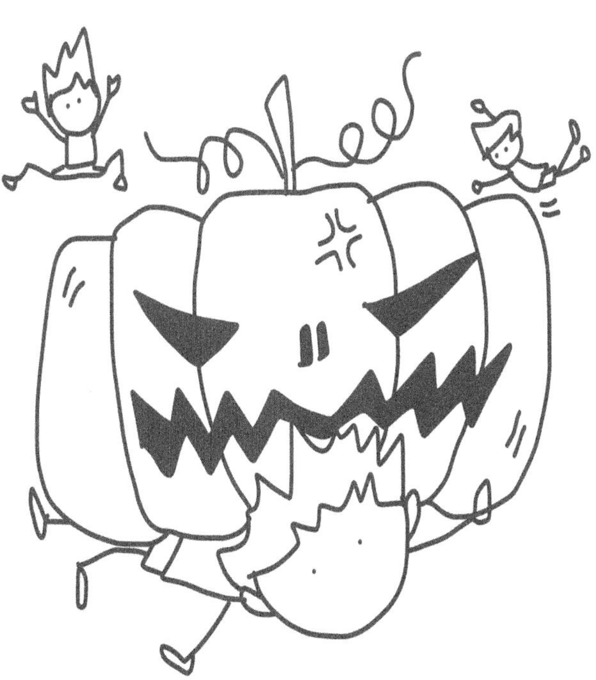

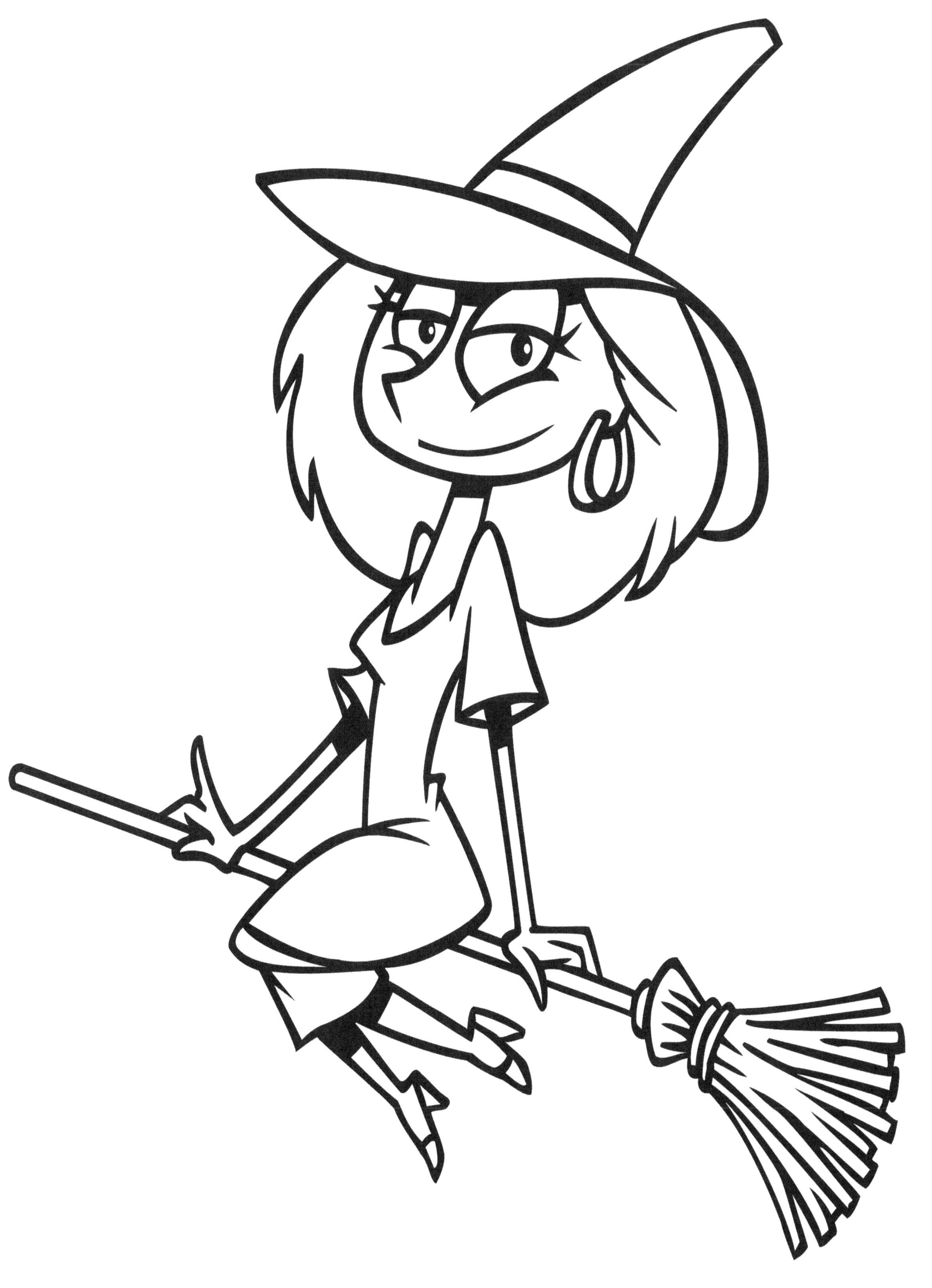

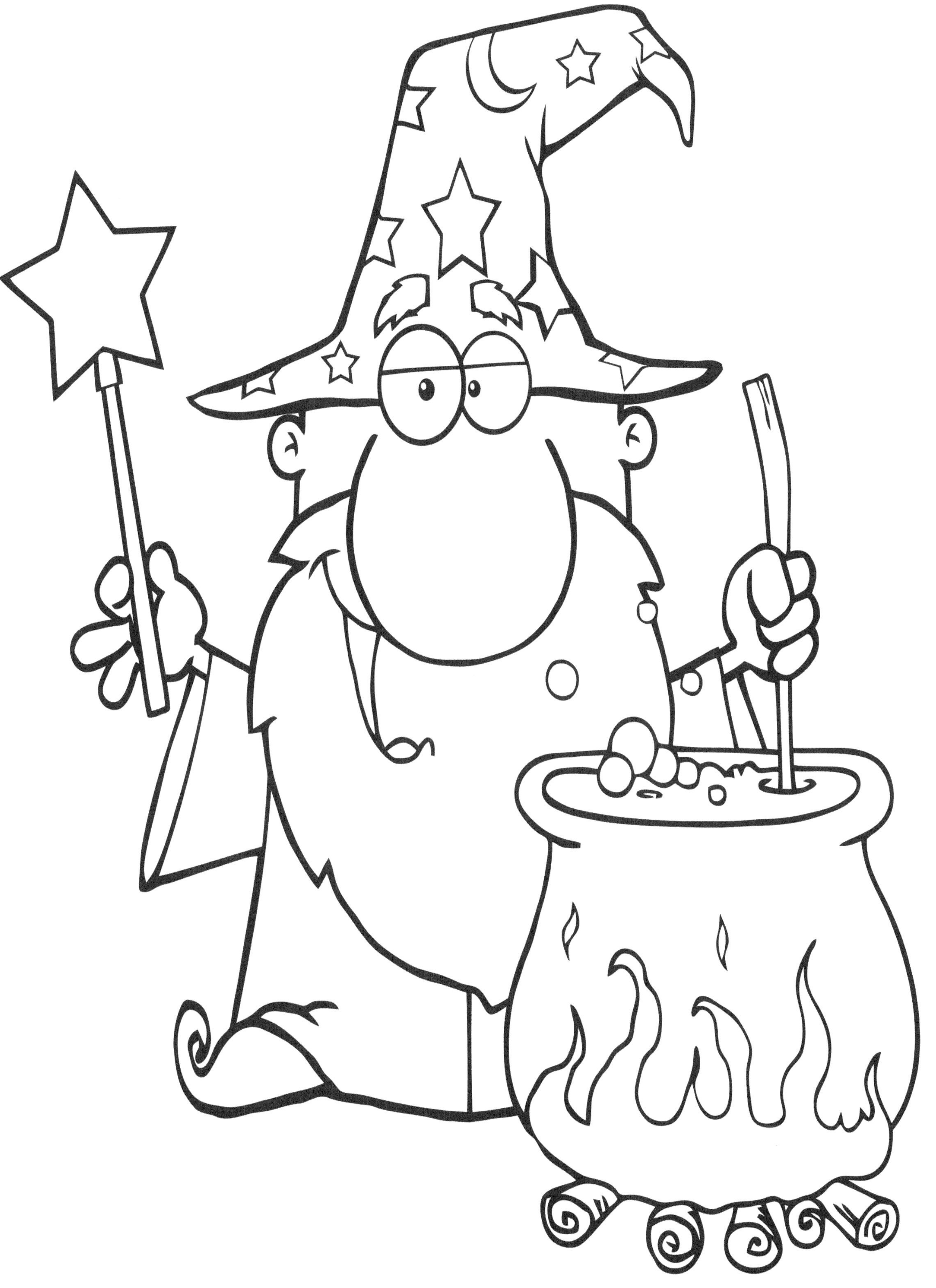

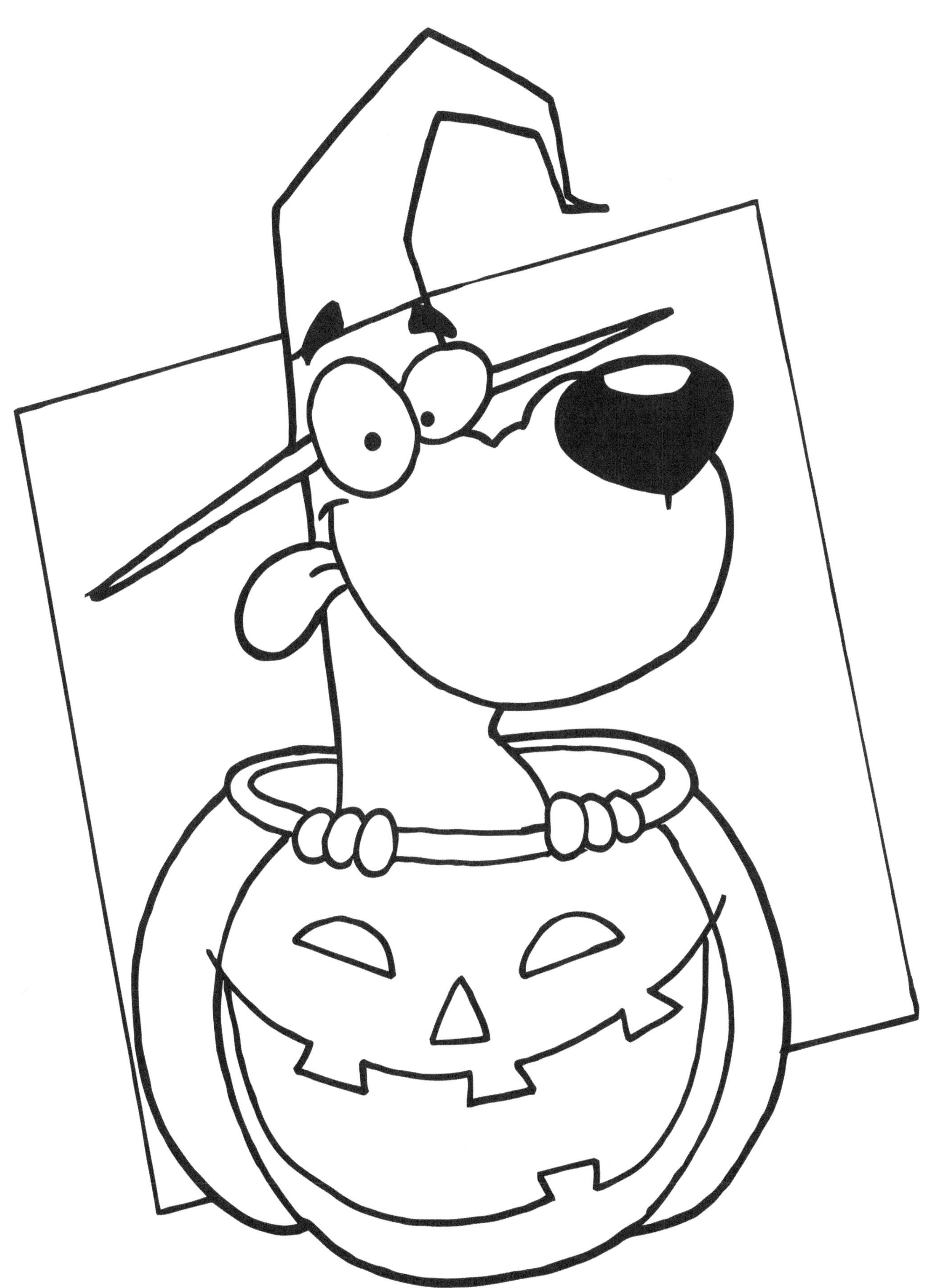

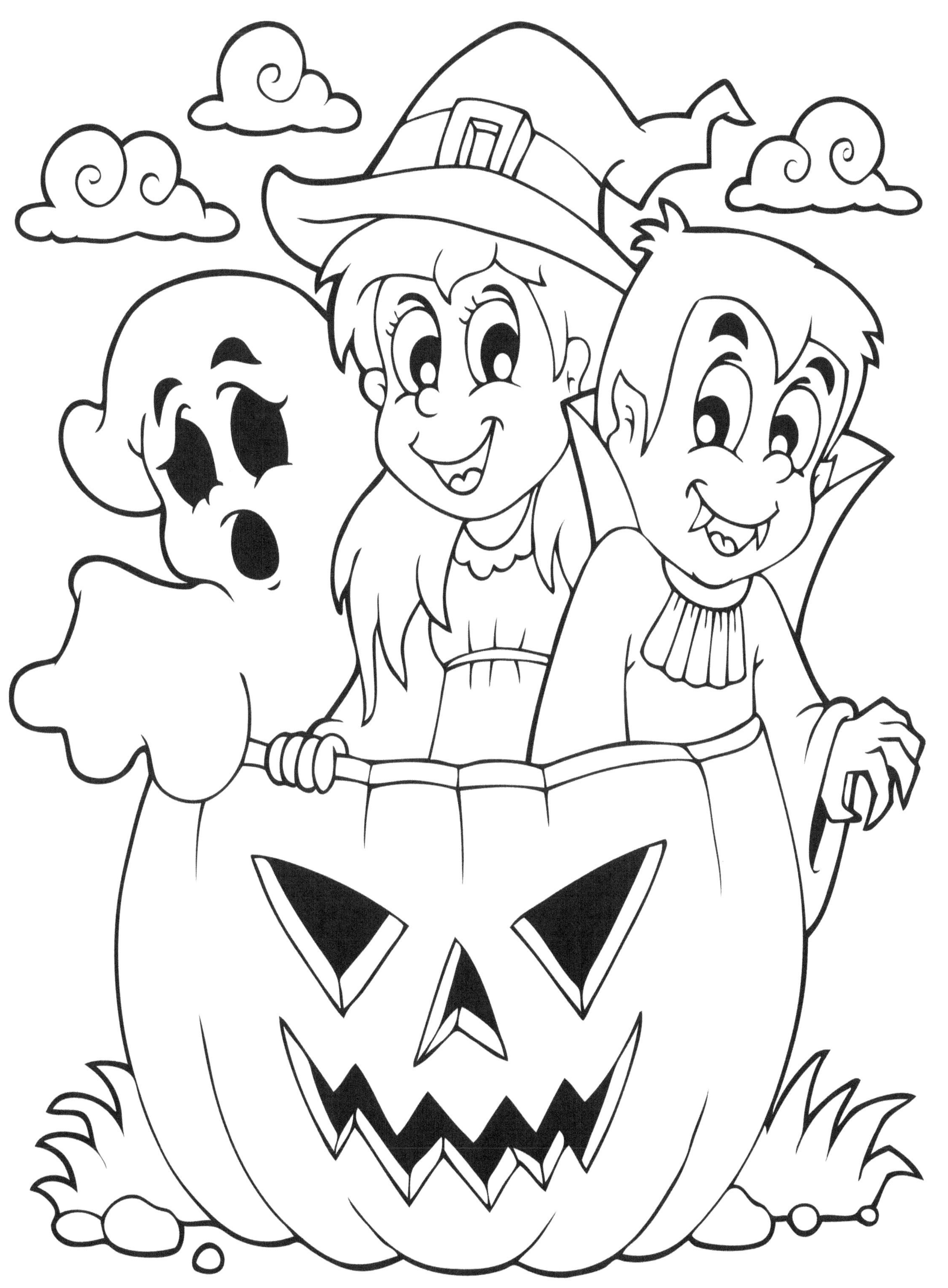

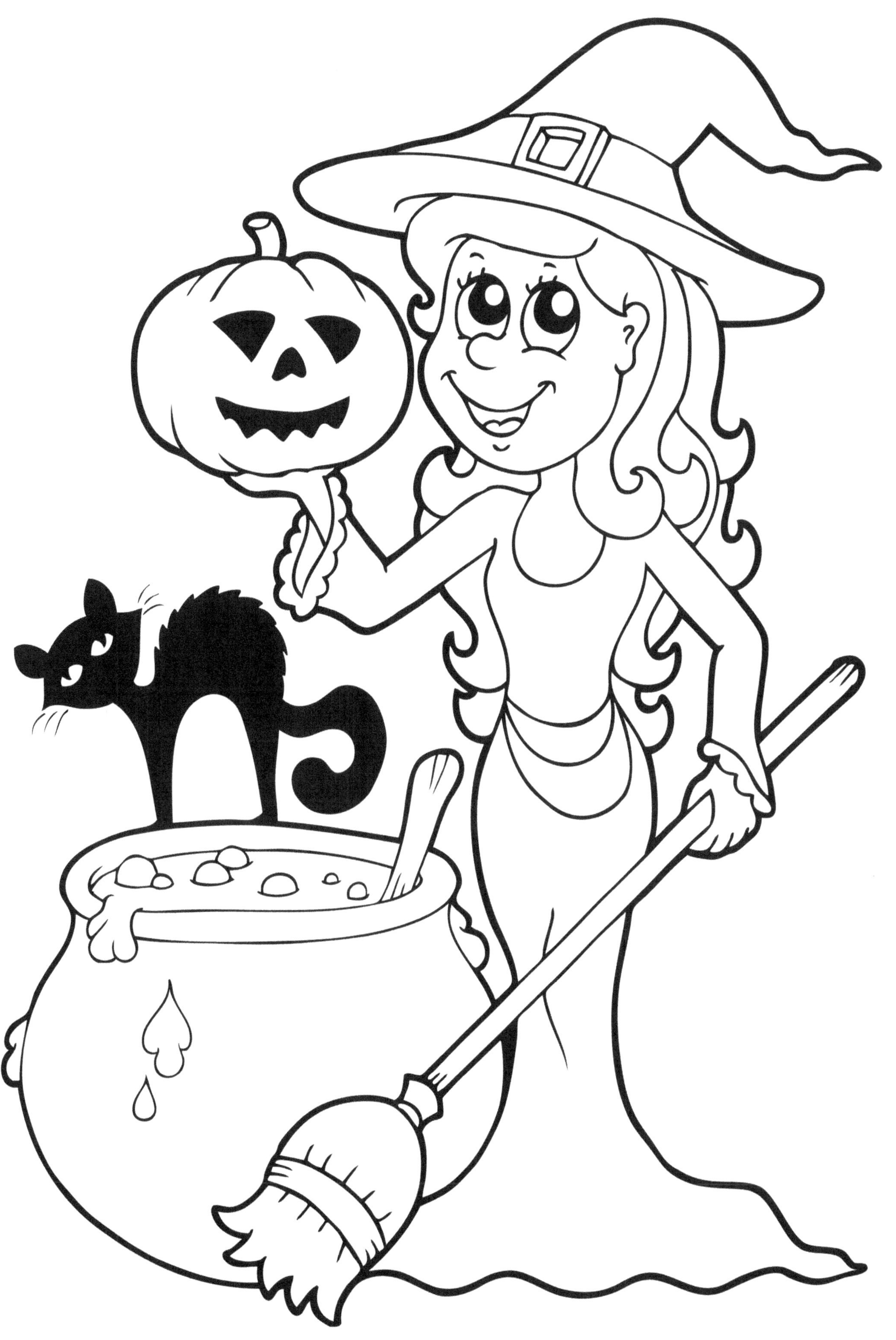

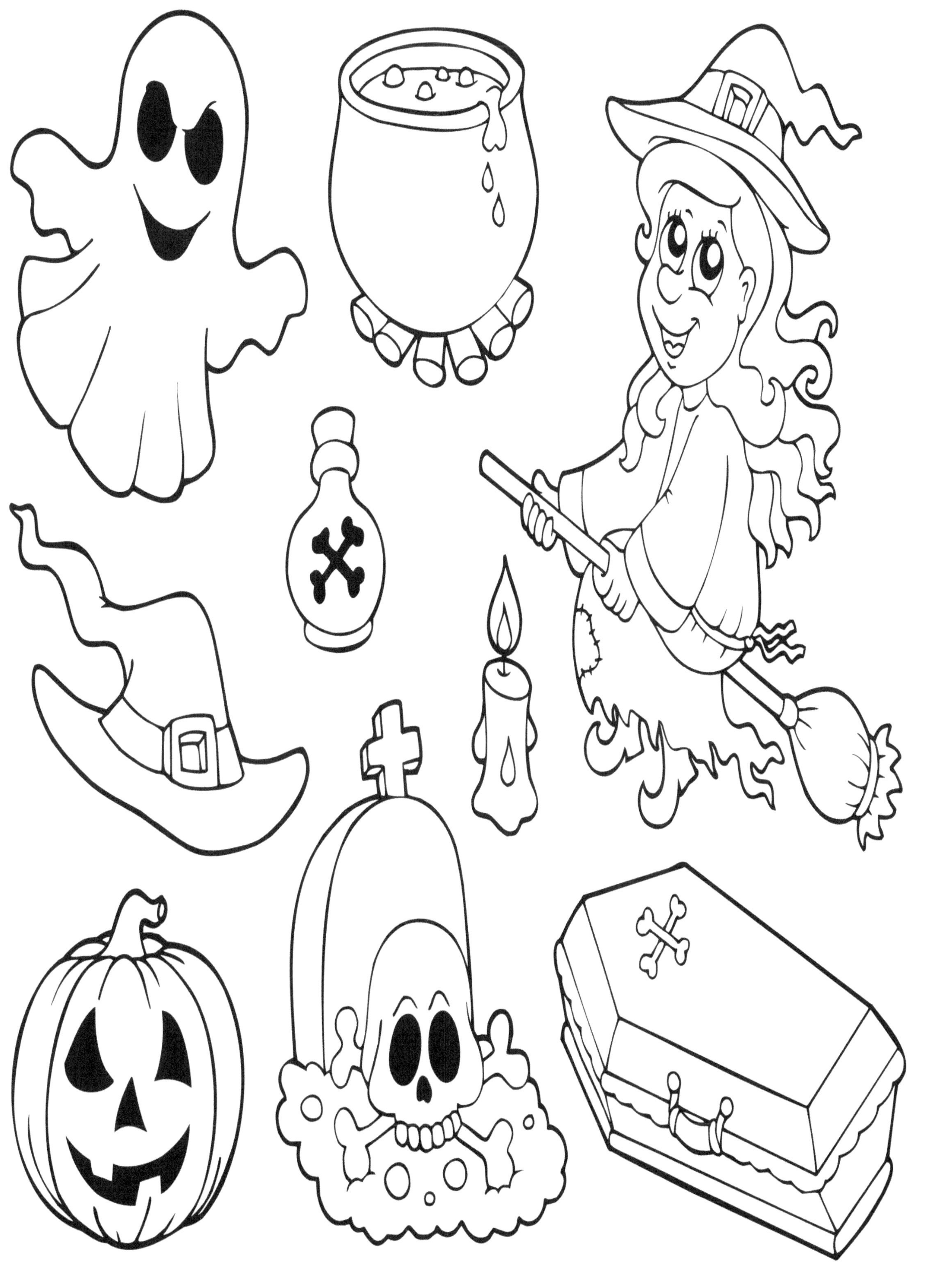

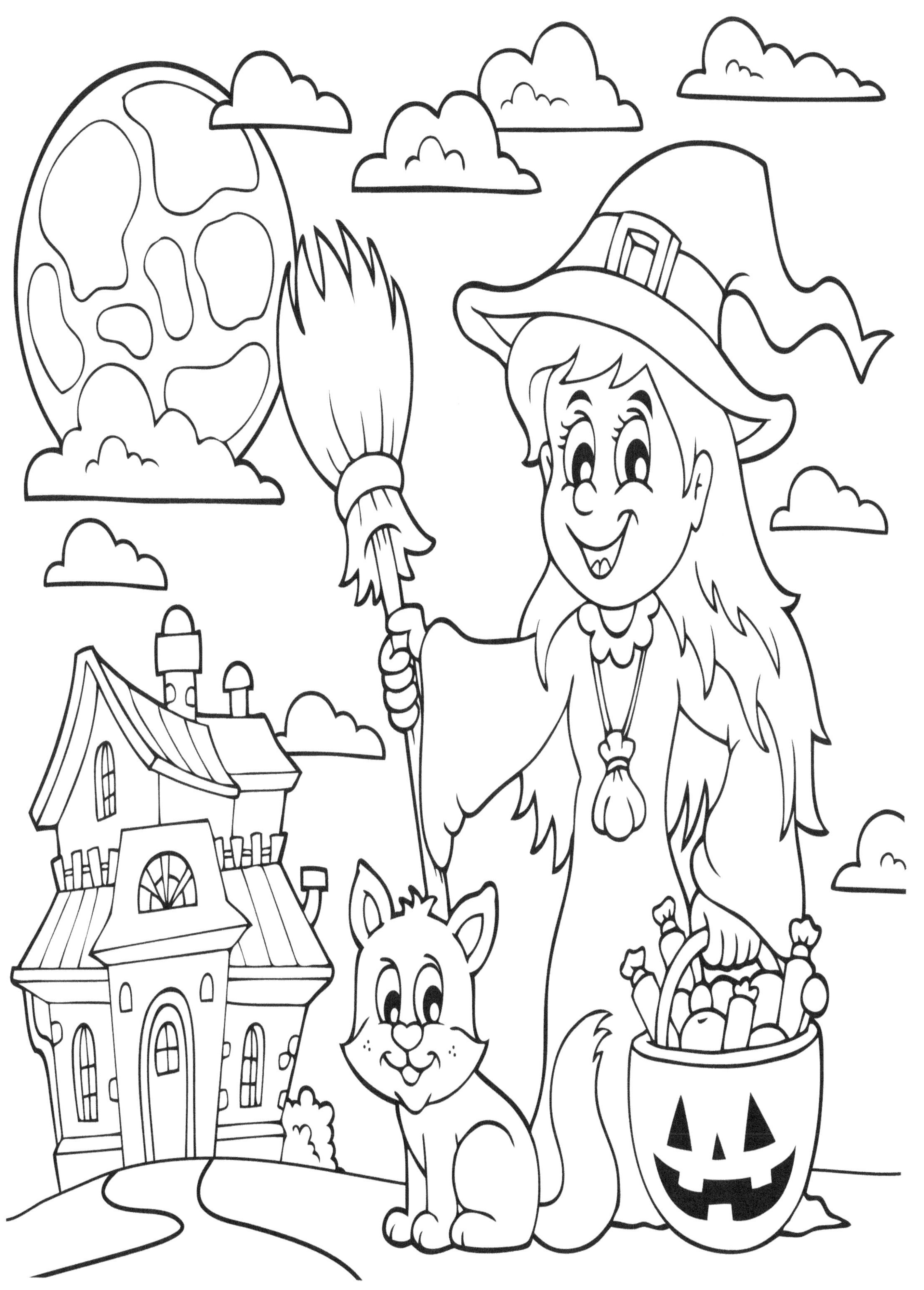

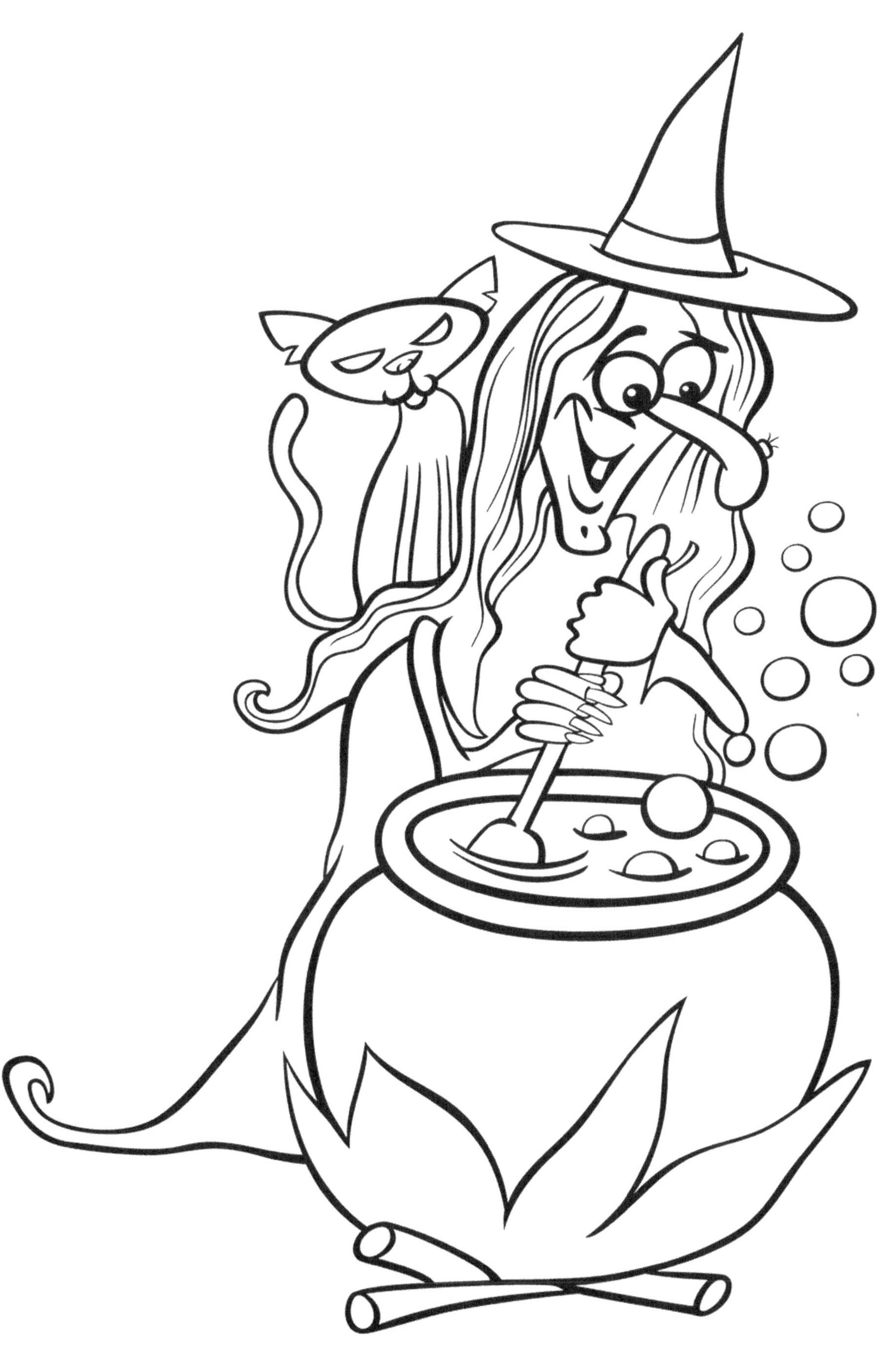

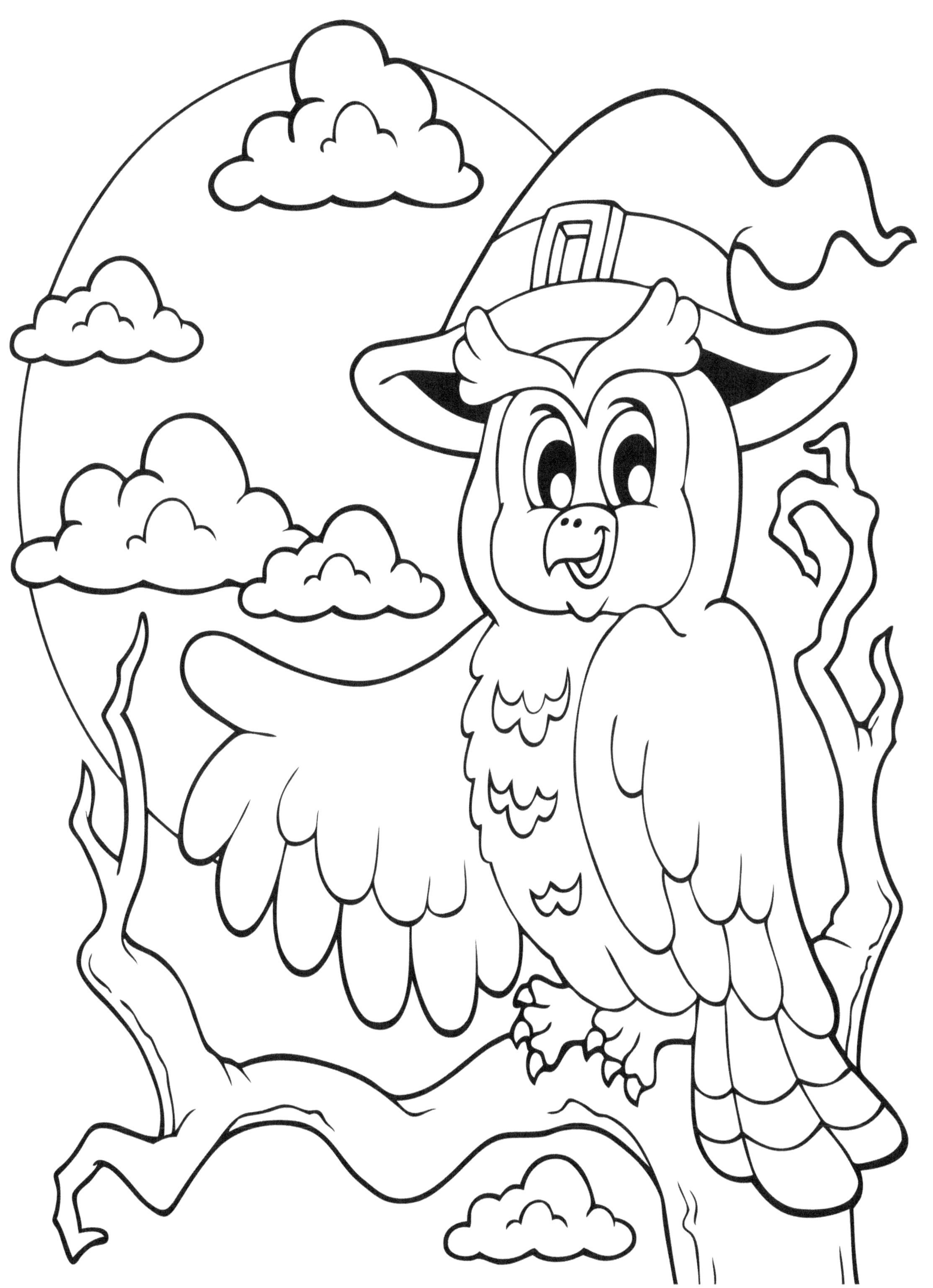

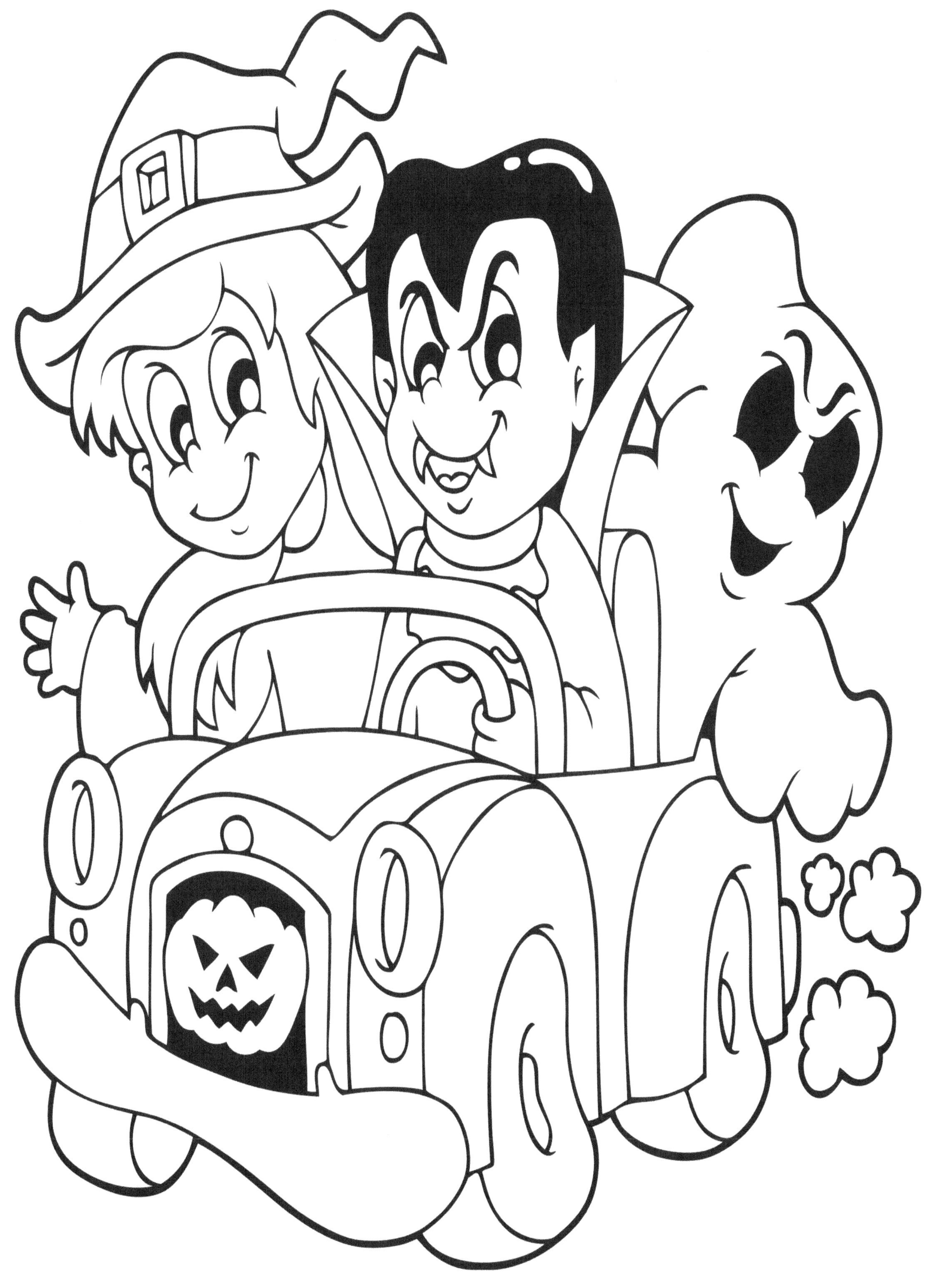

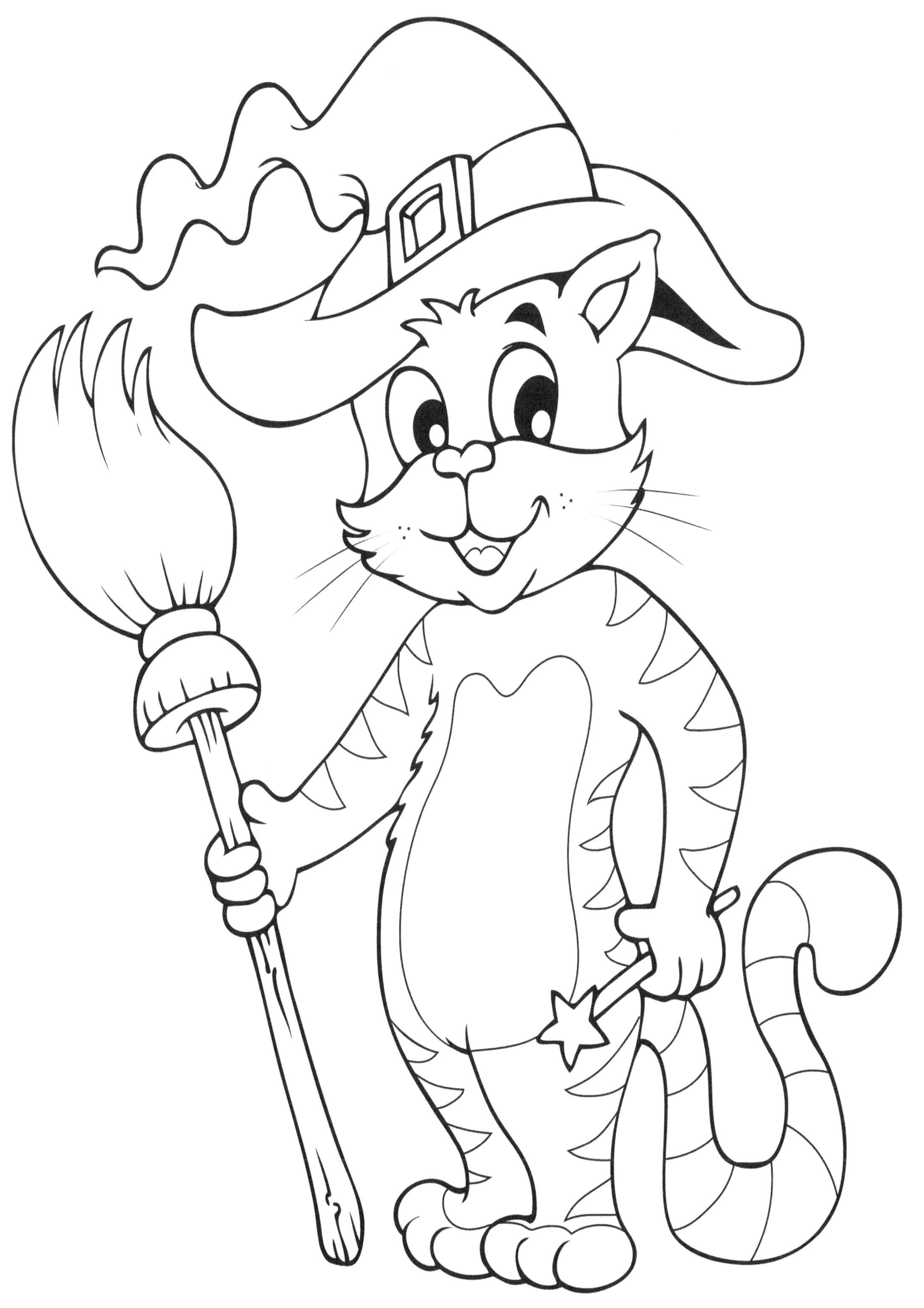

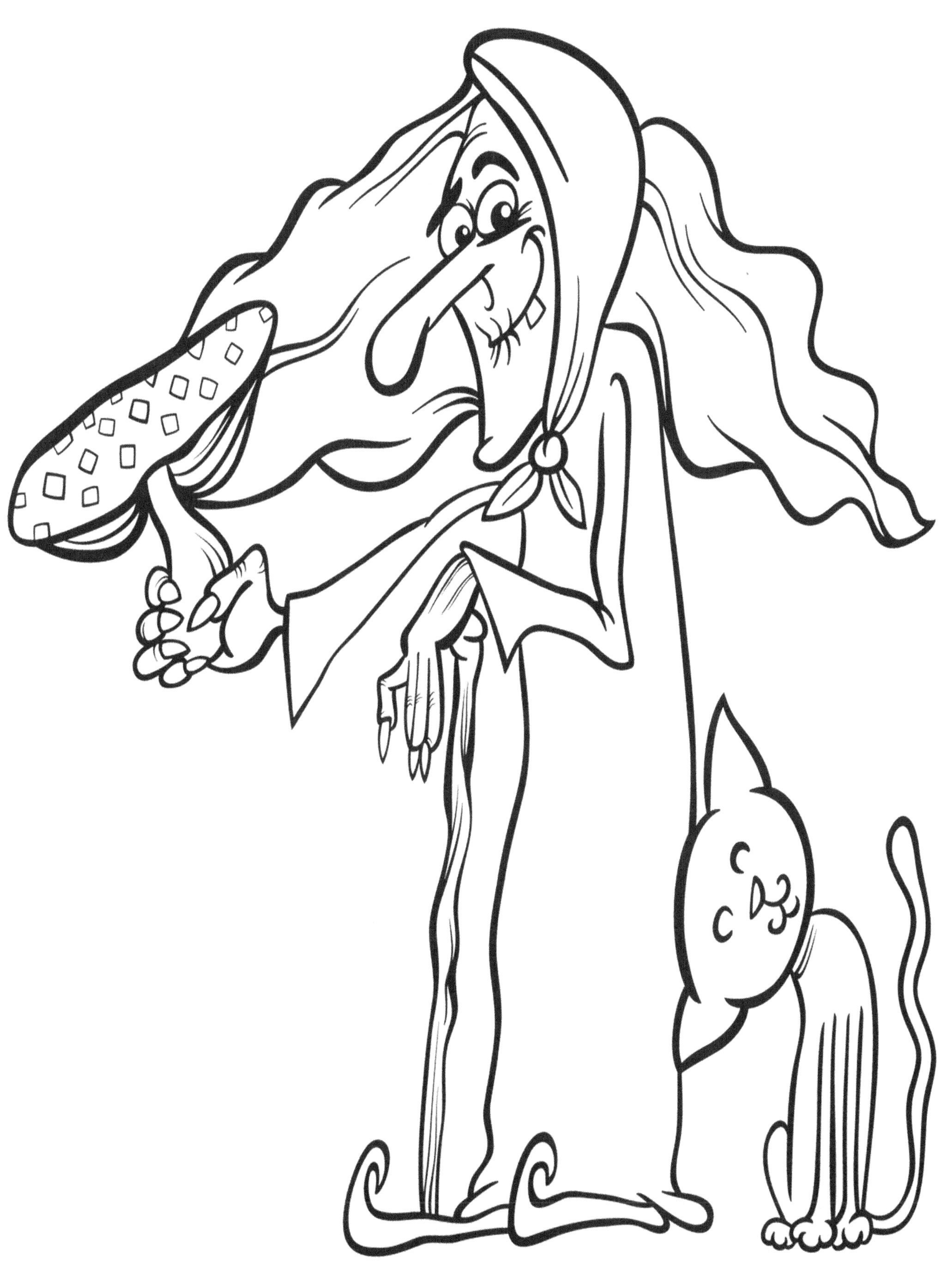

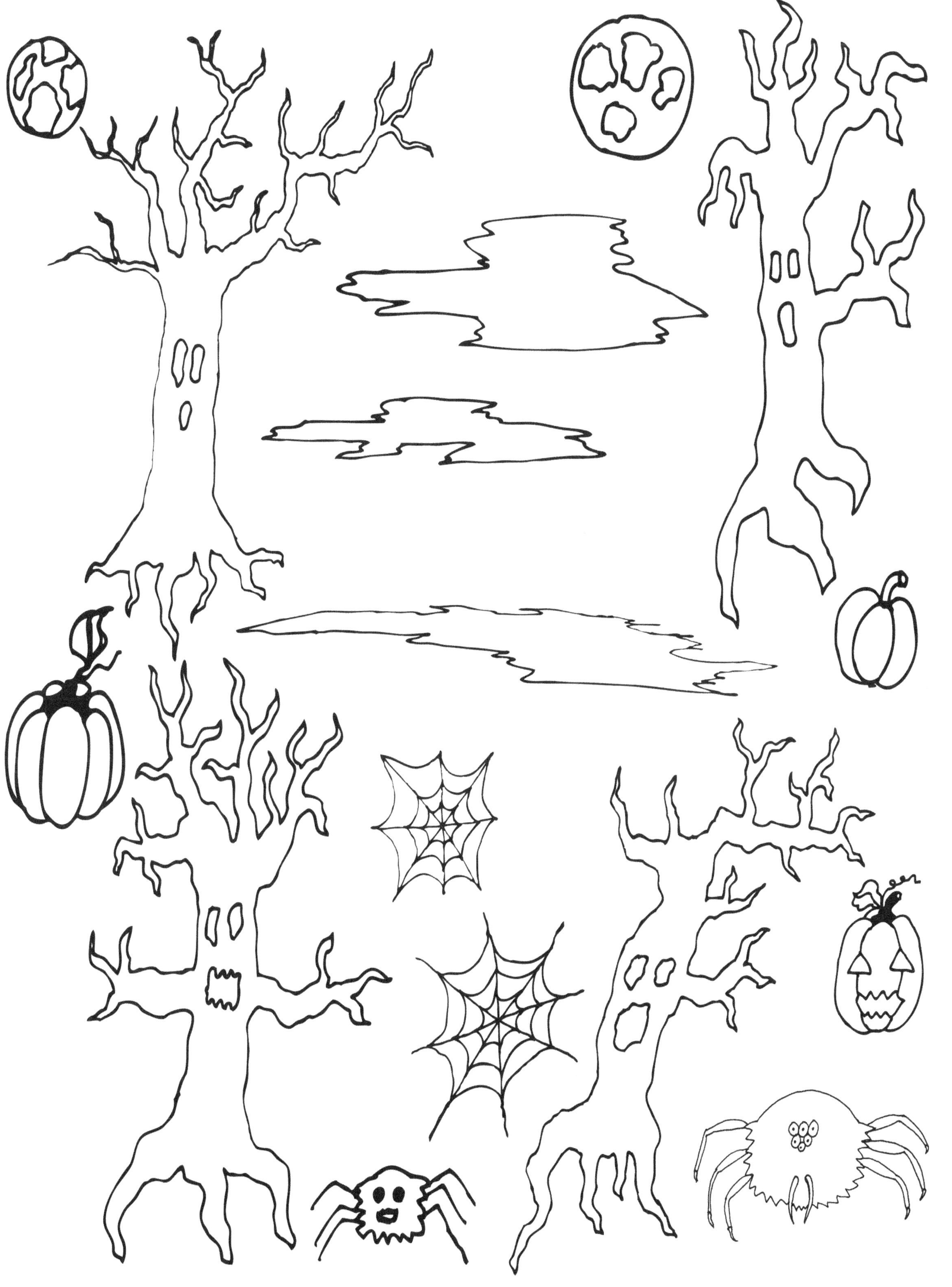

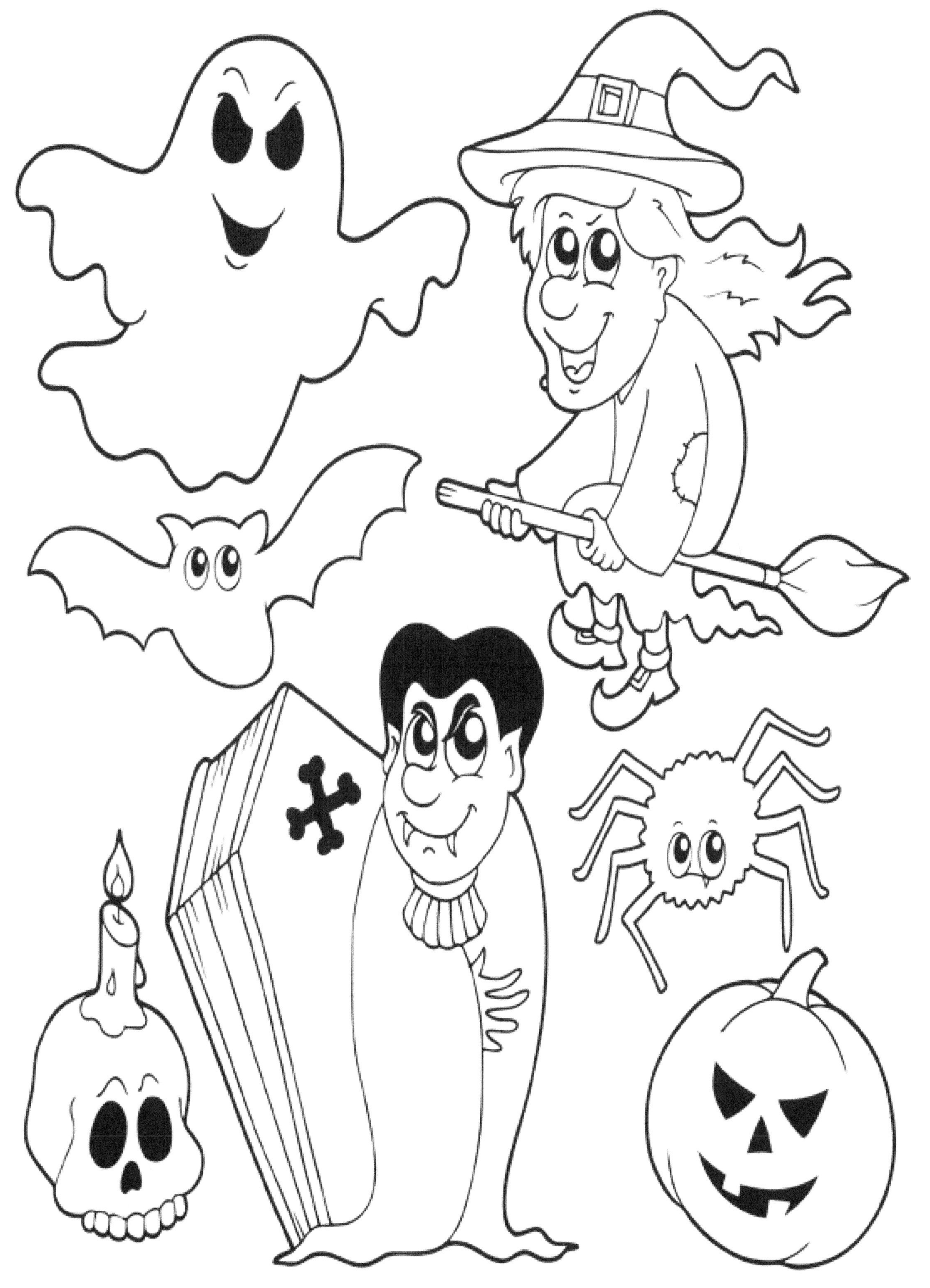

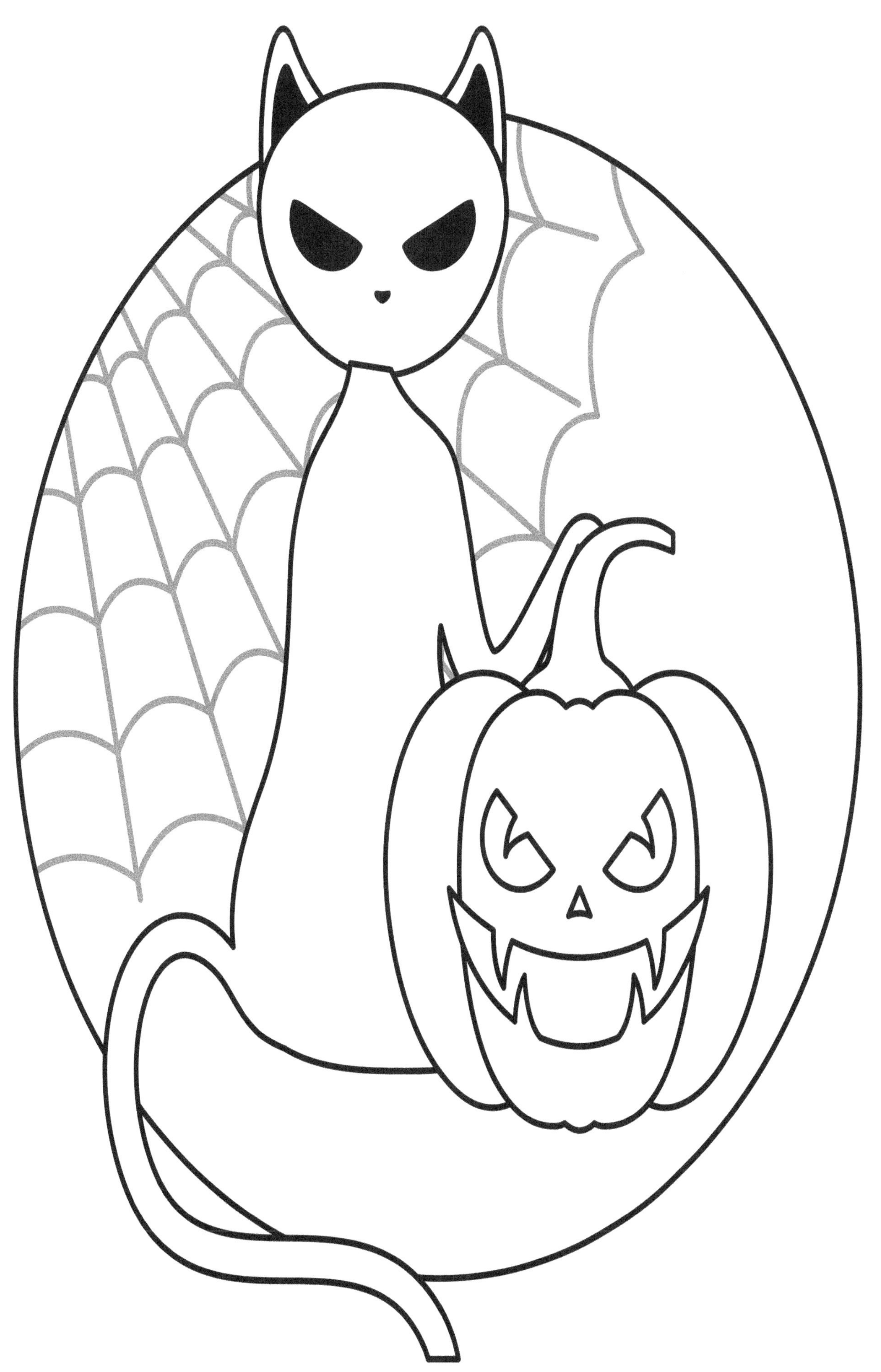

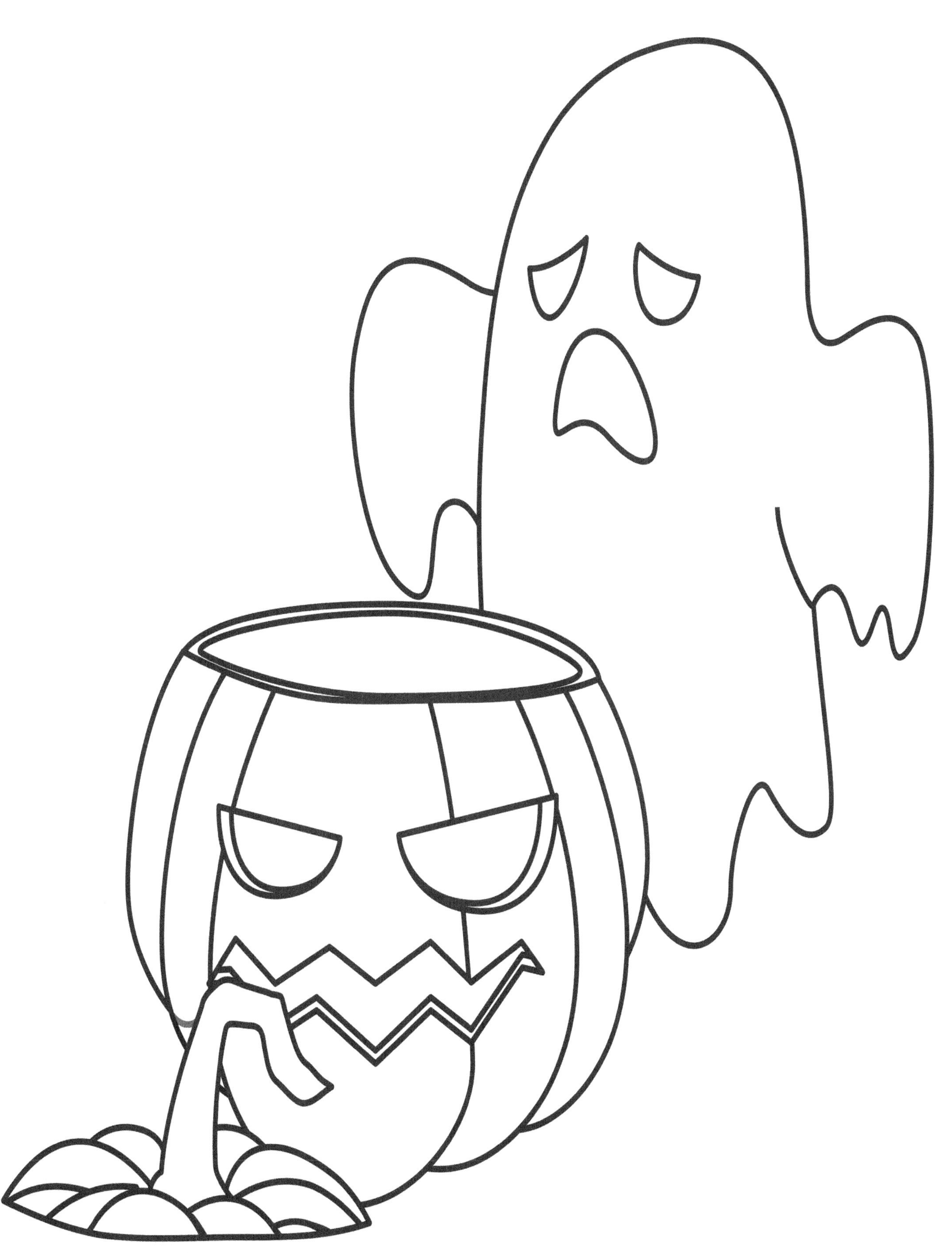

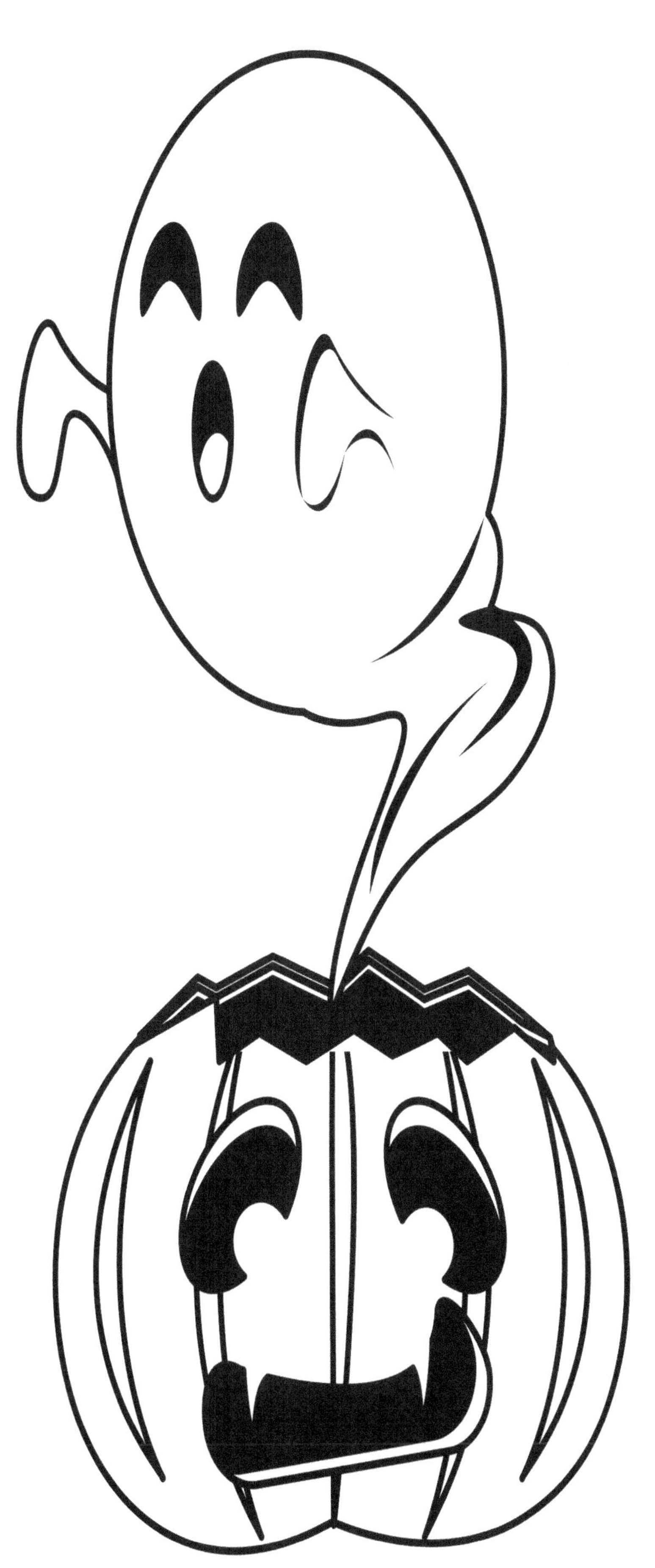

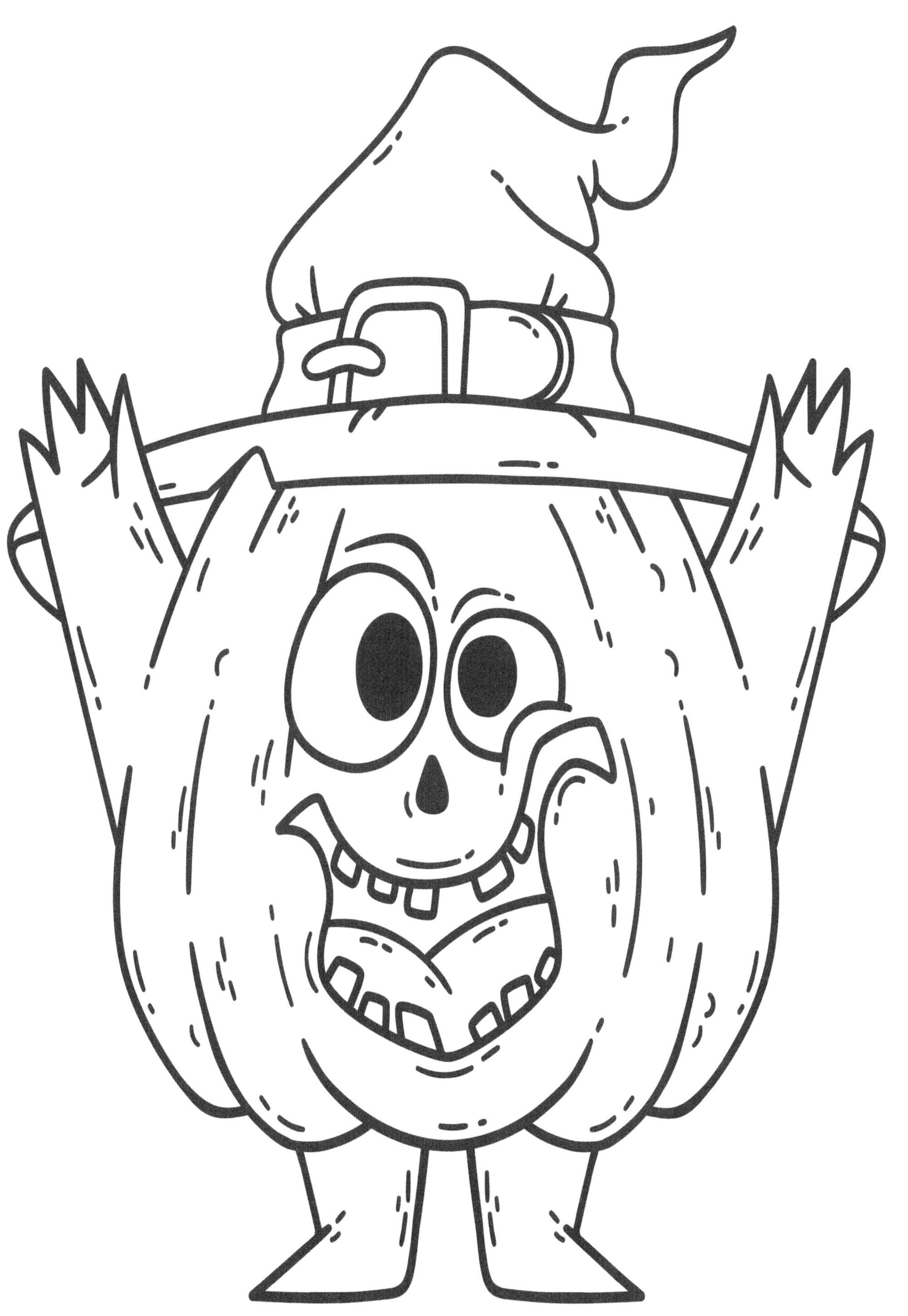

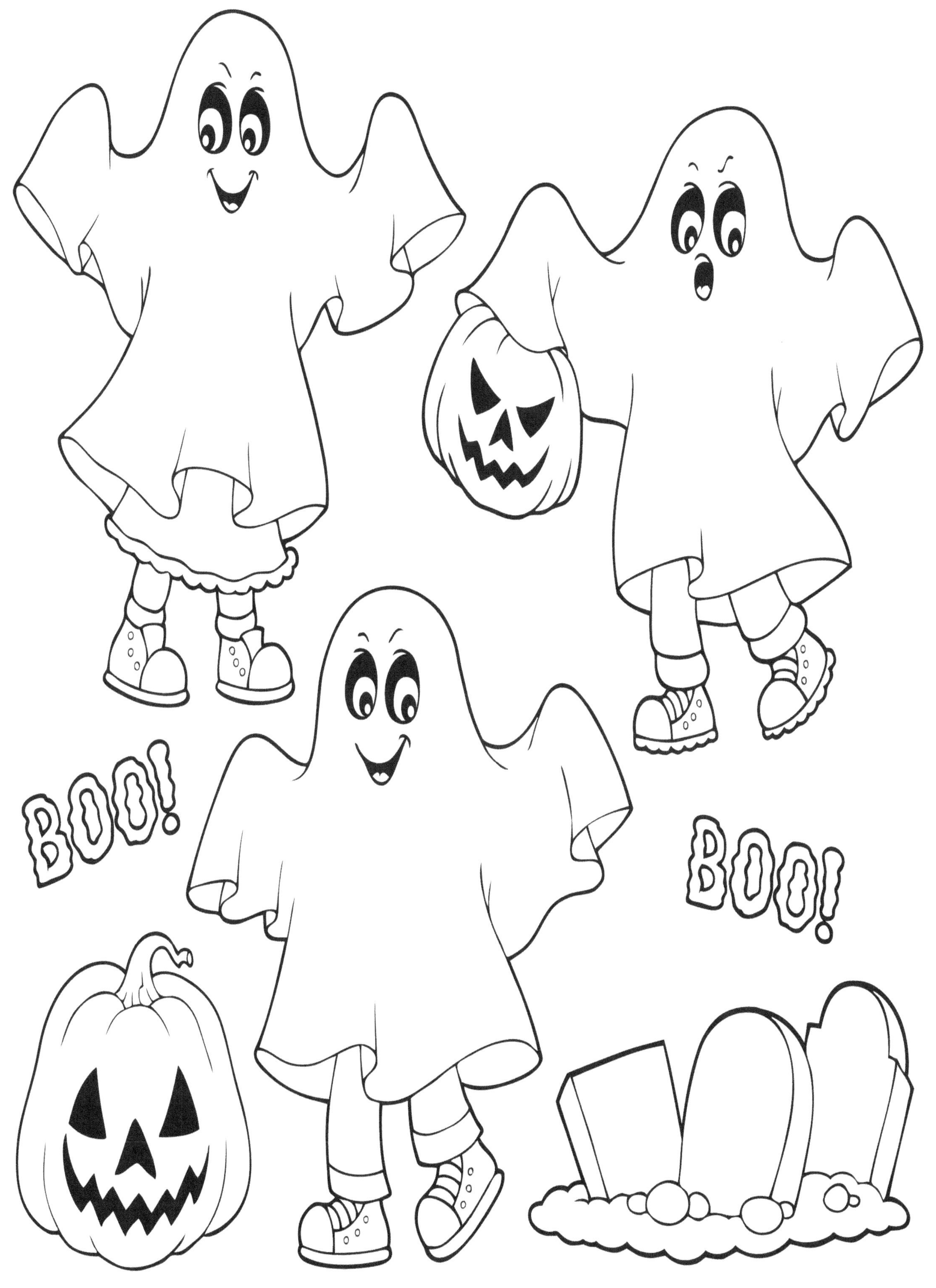
BOO!
BOO!

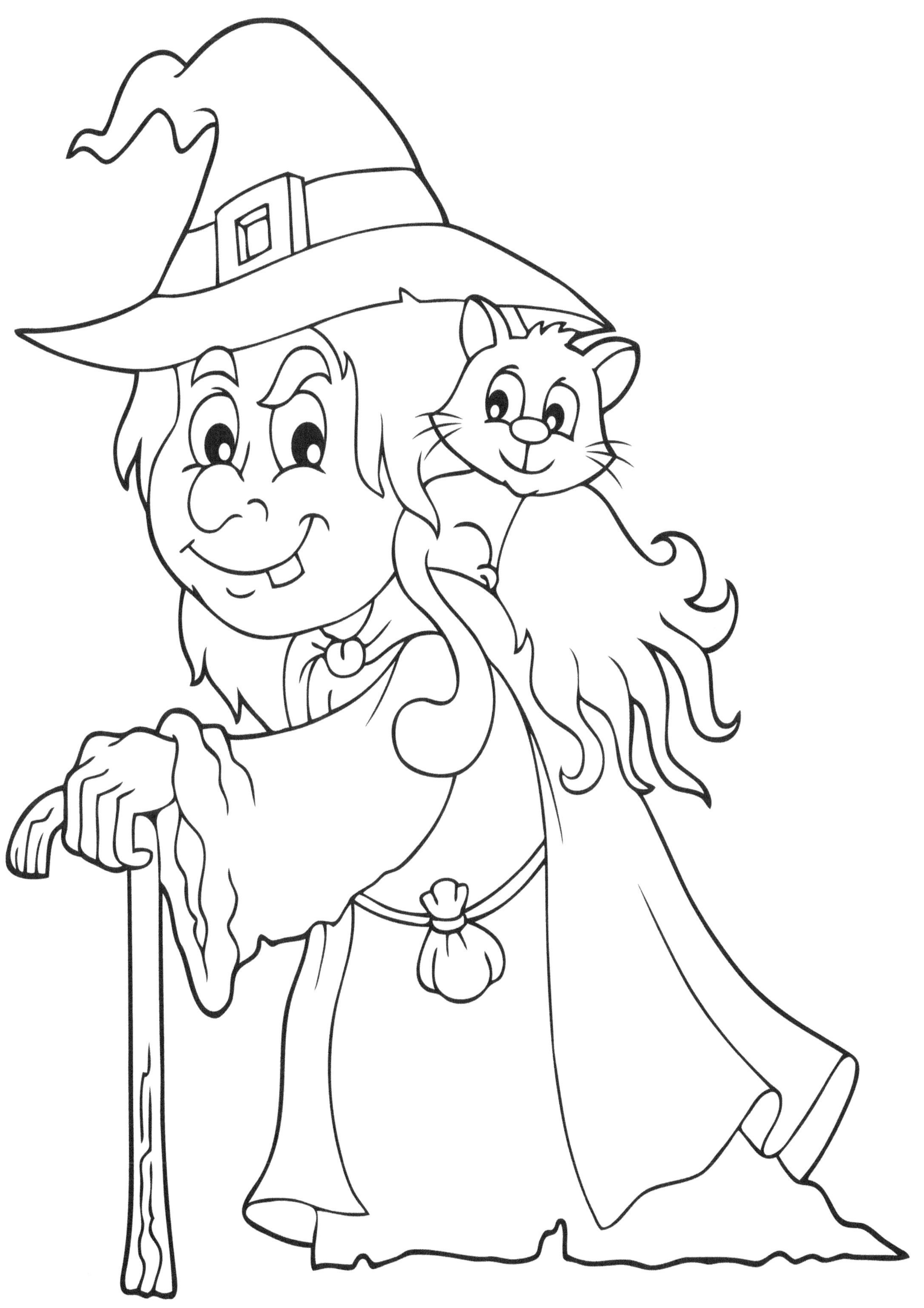

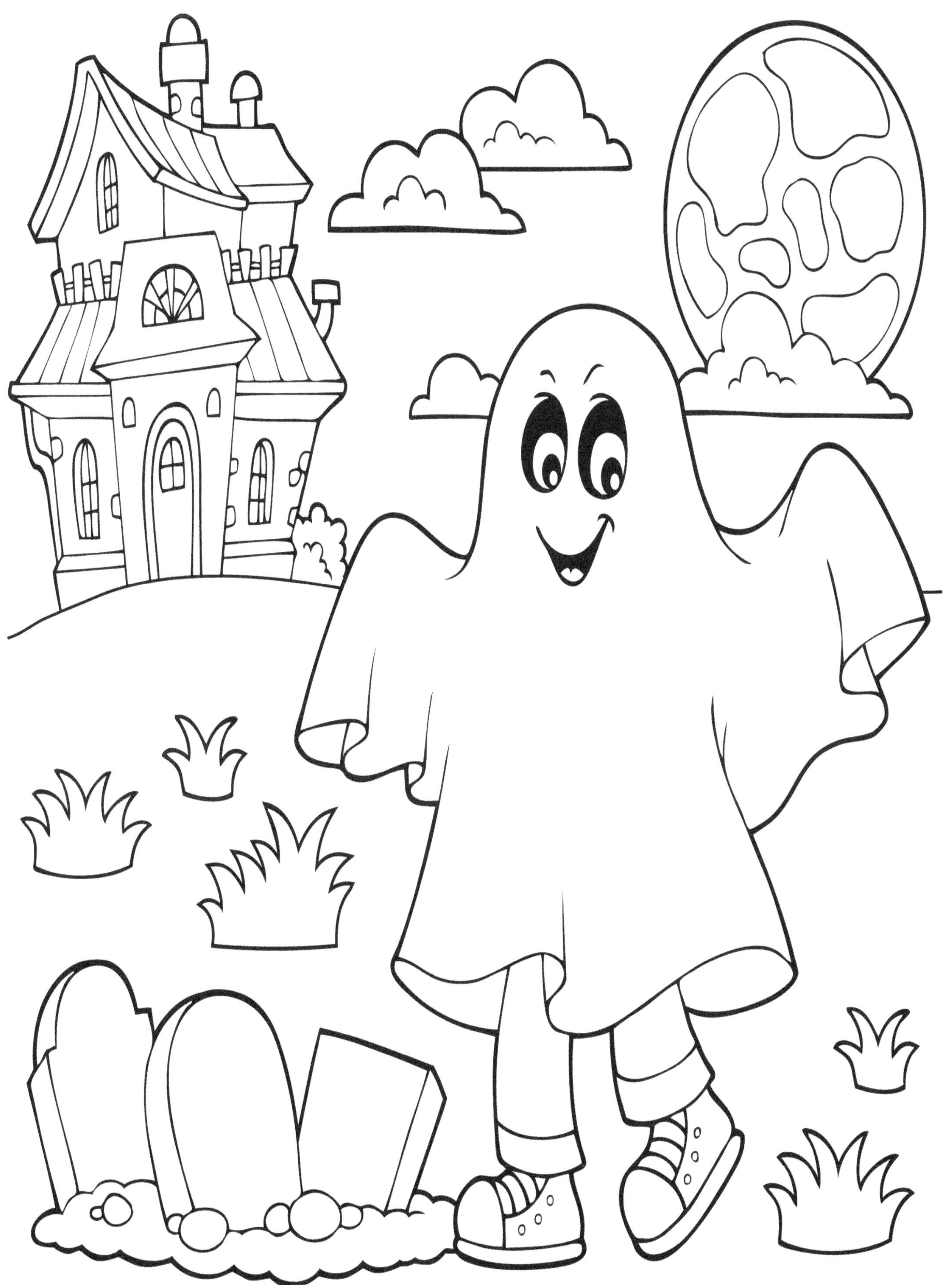

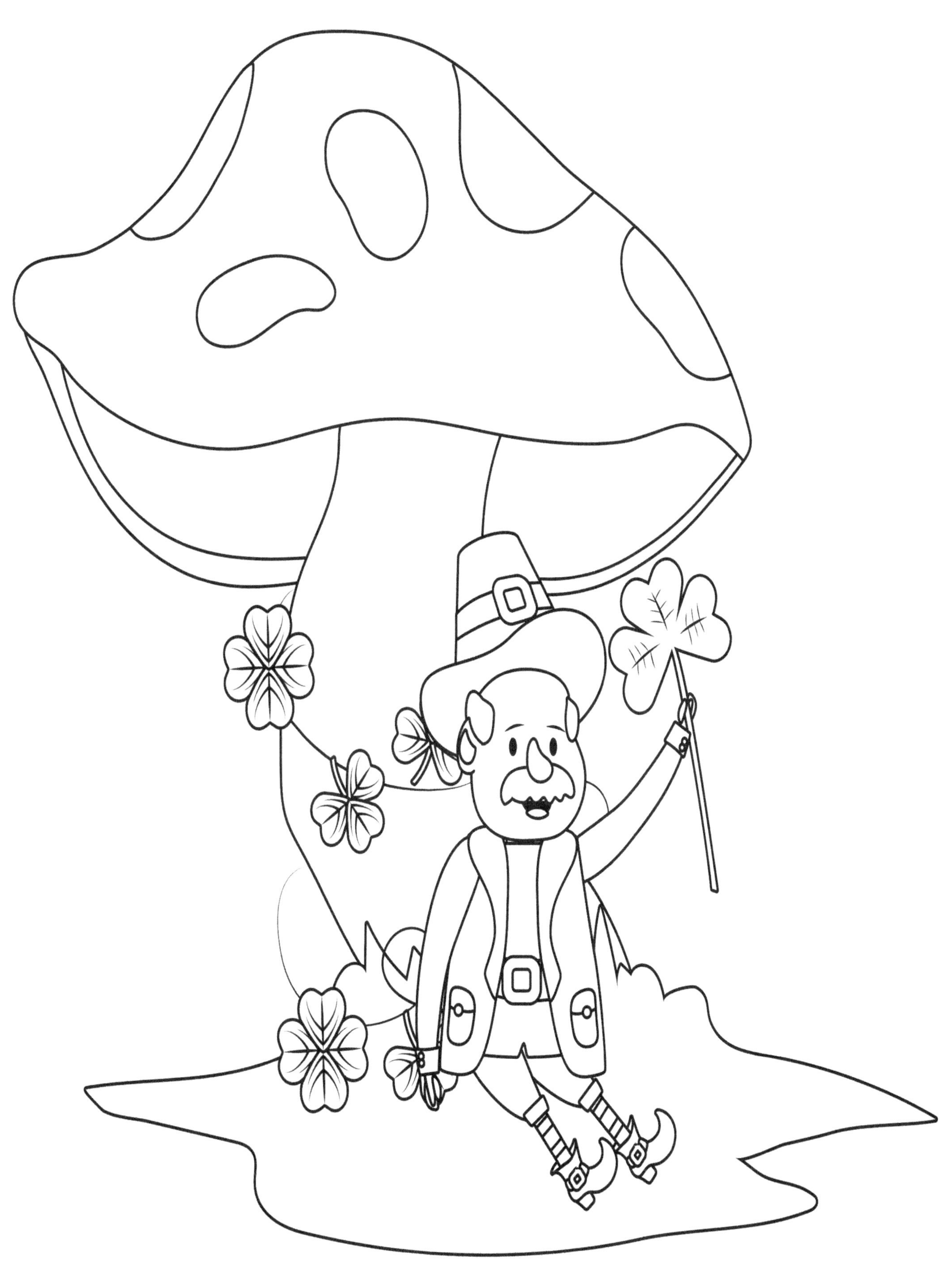

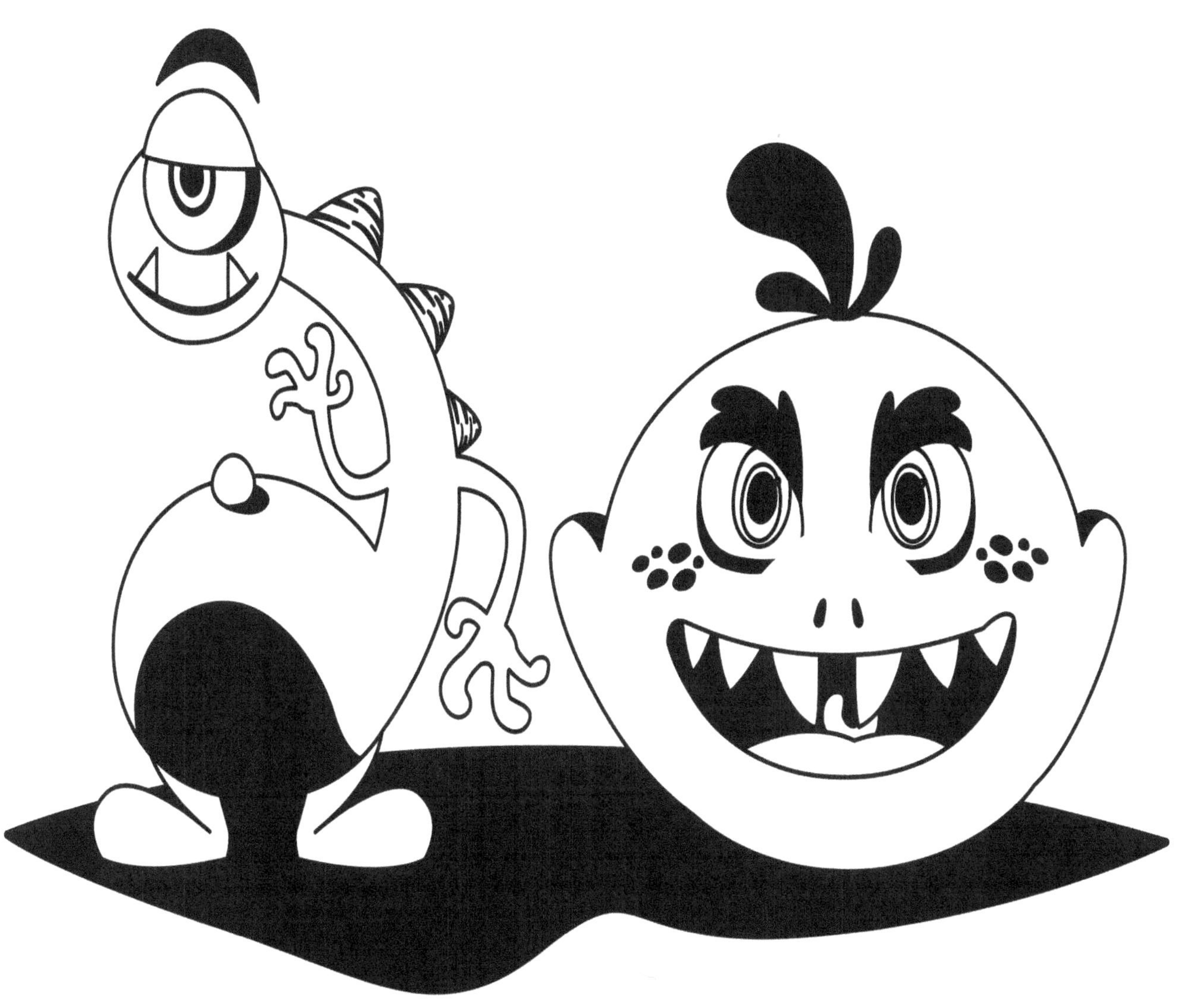

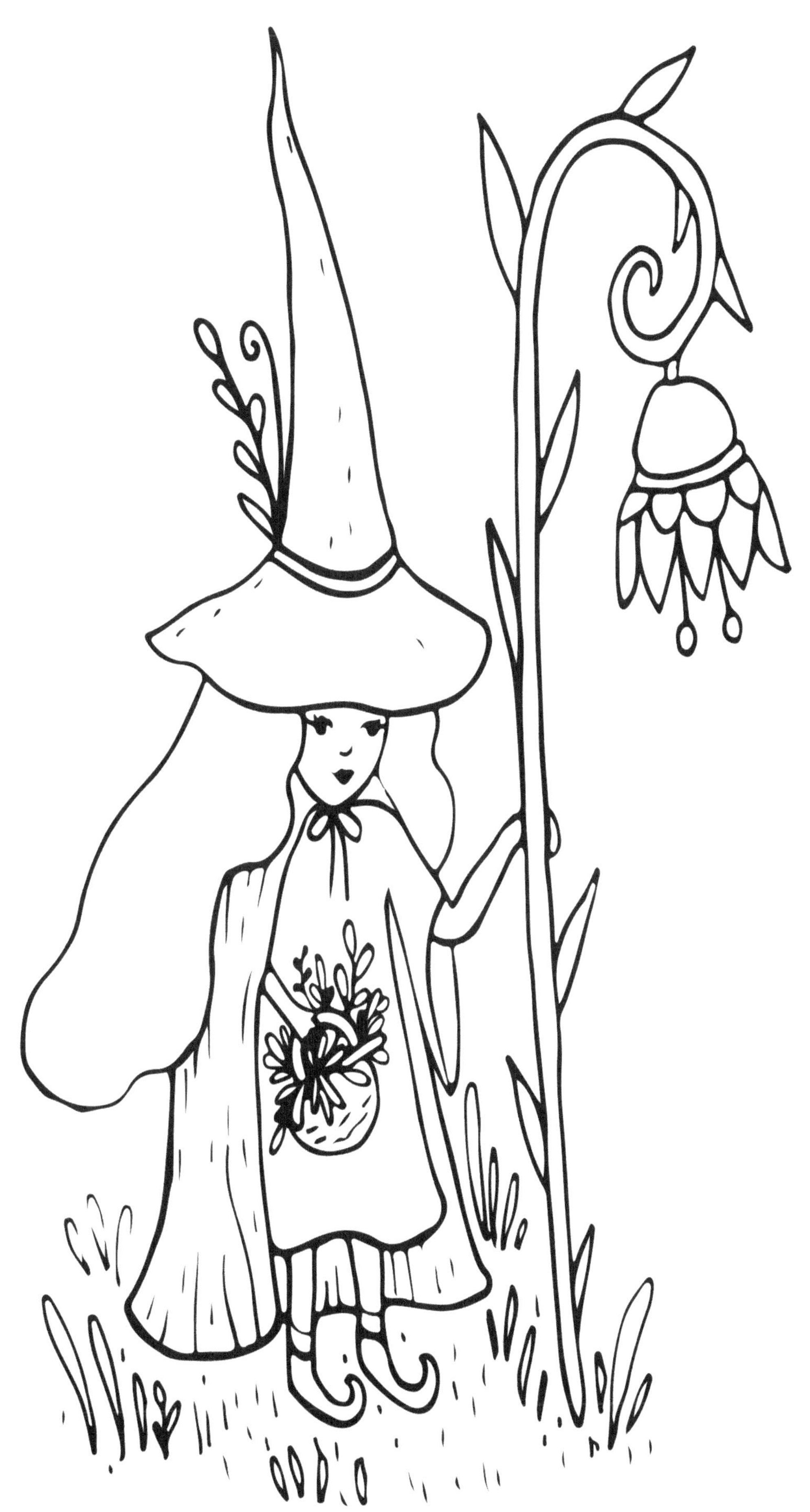

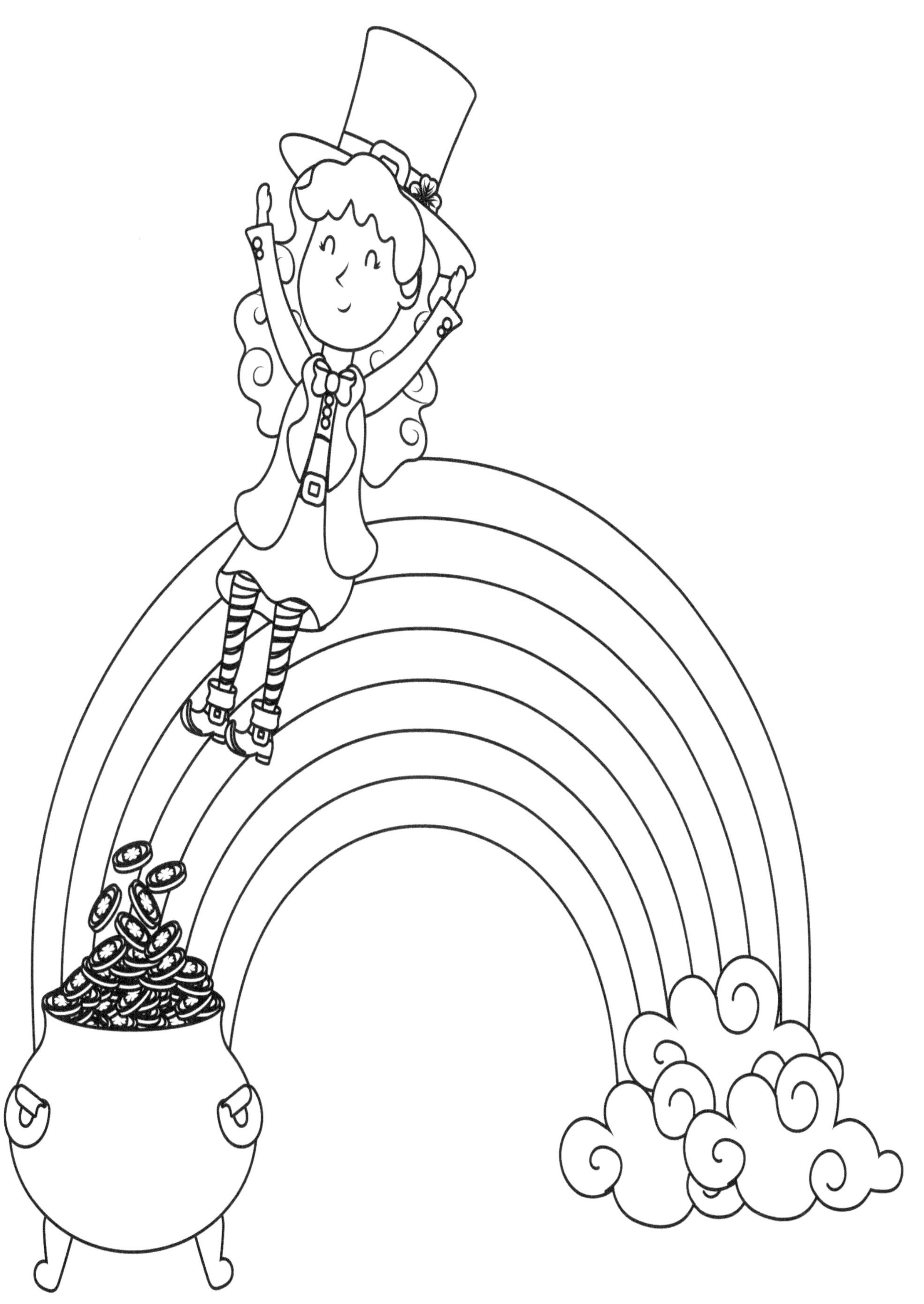

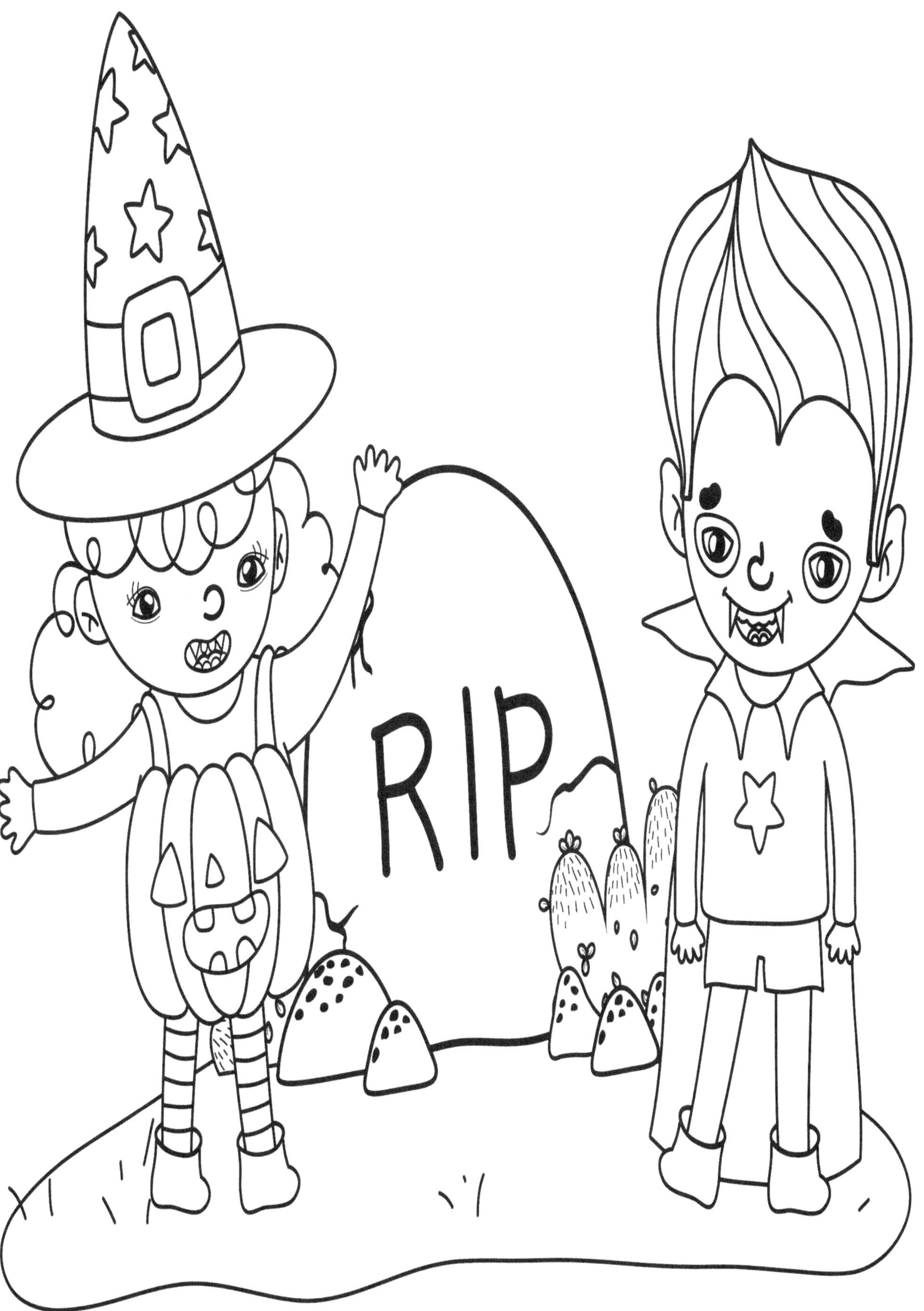

RIP

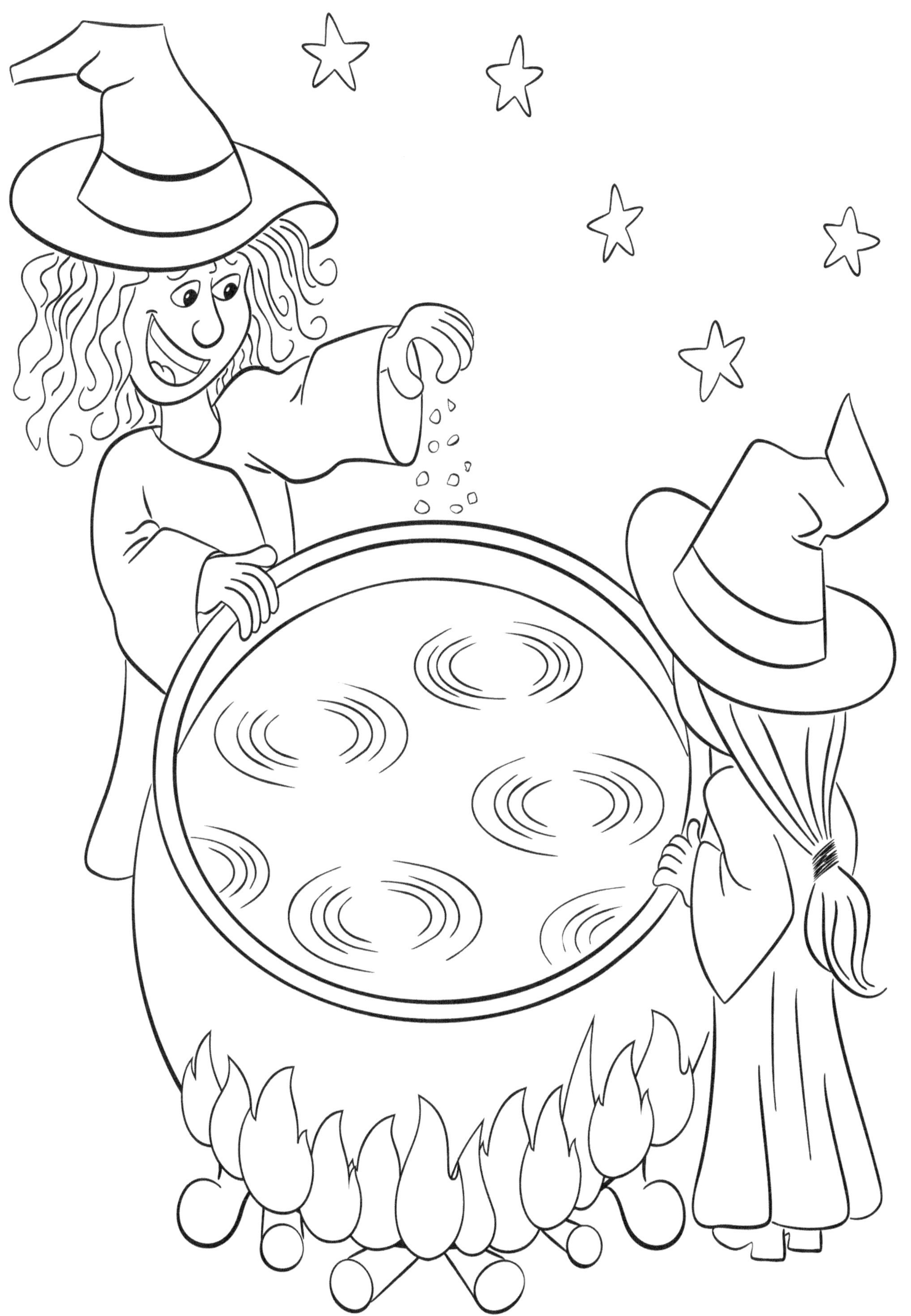

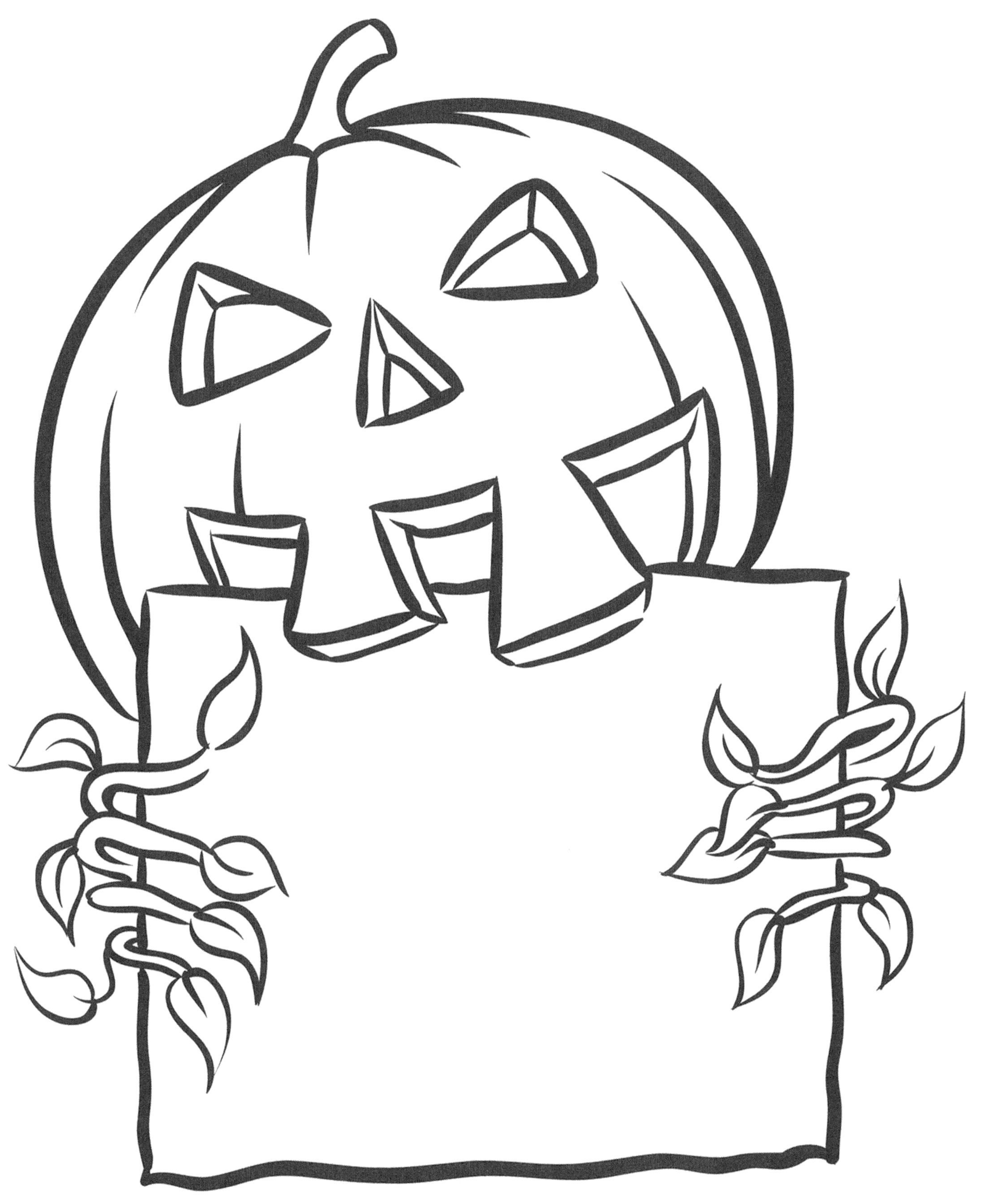

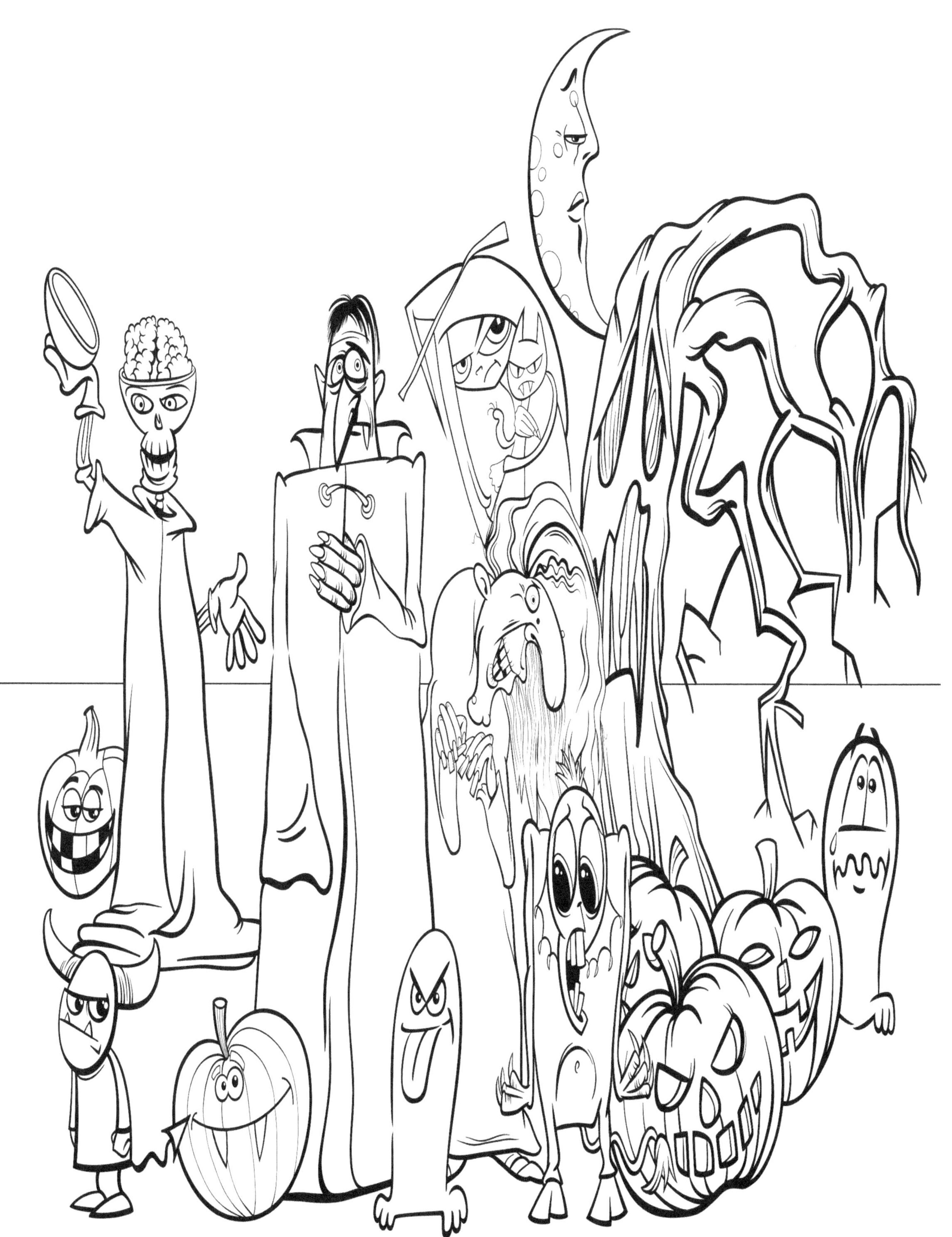

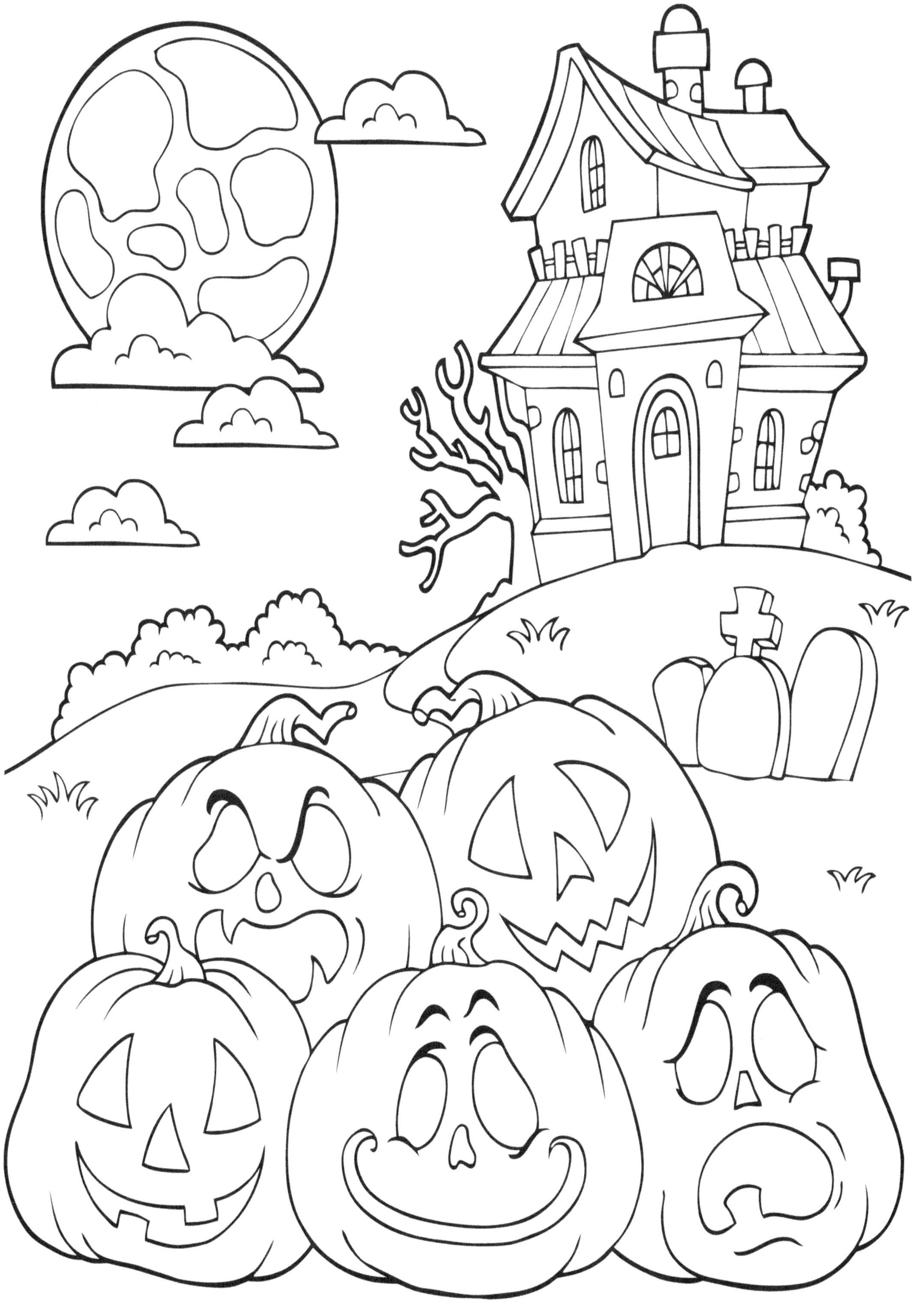

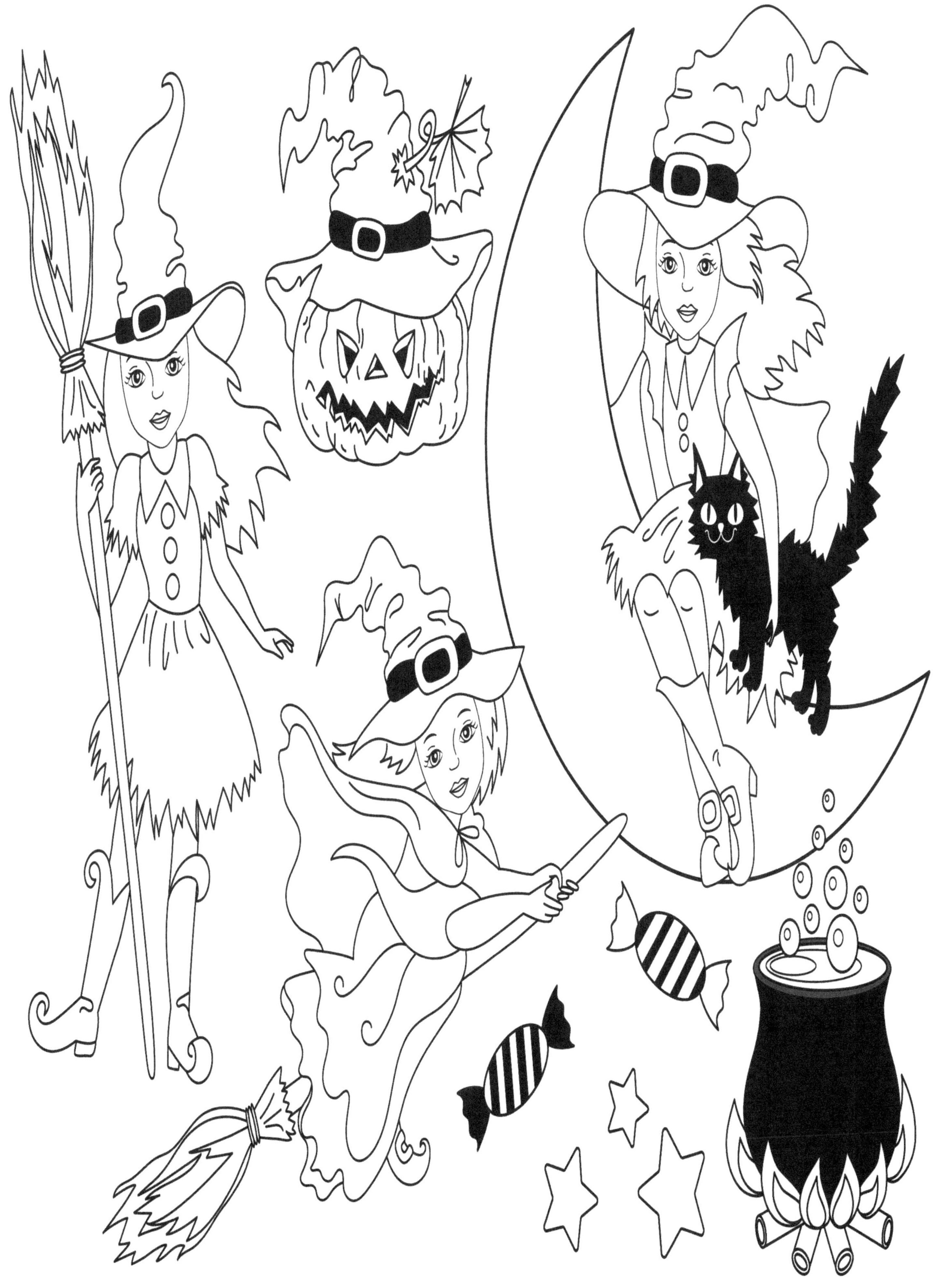

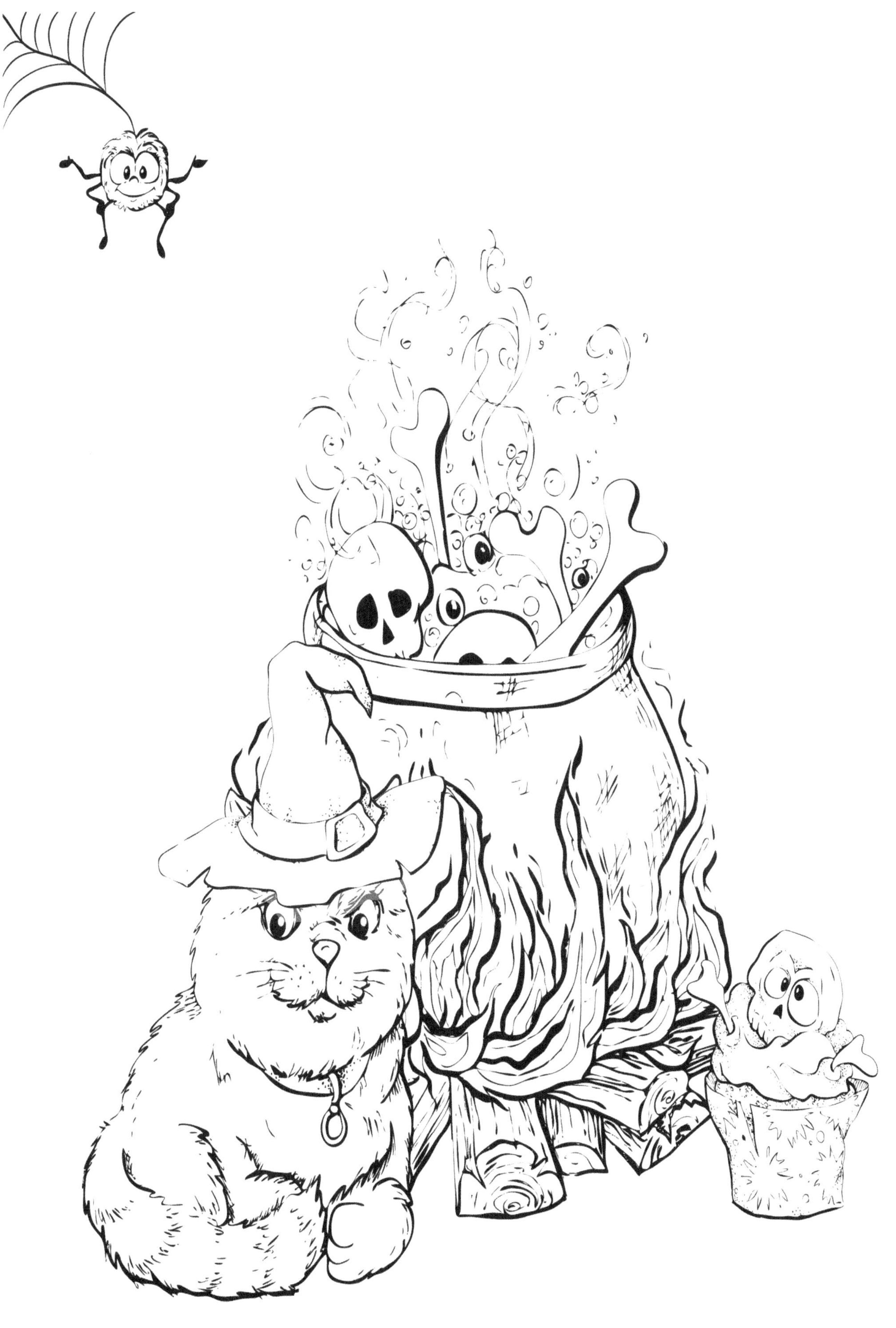

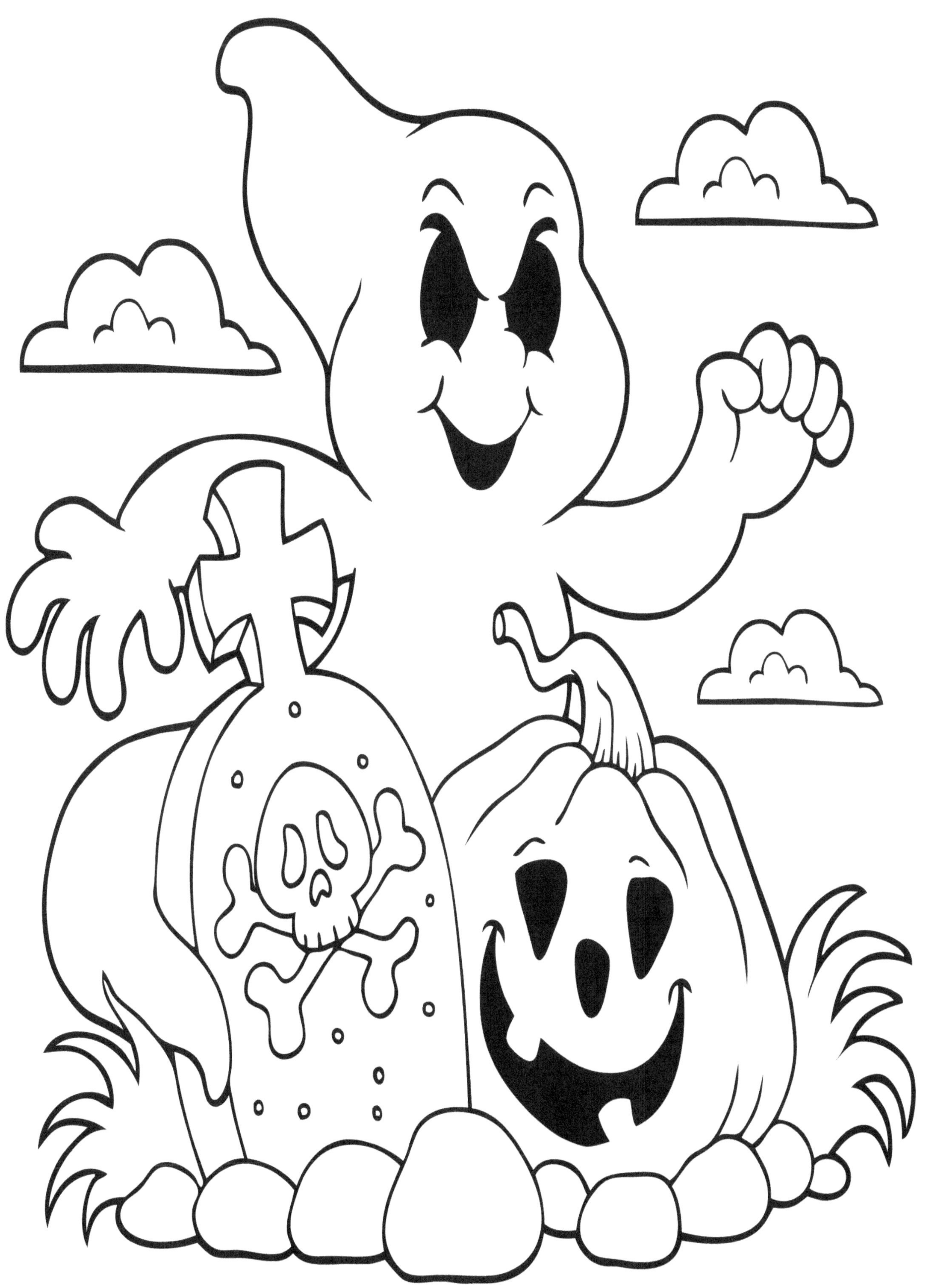

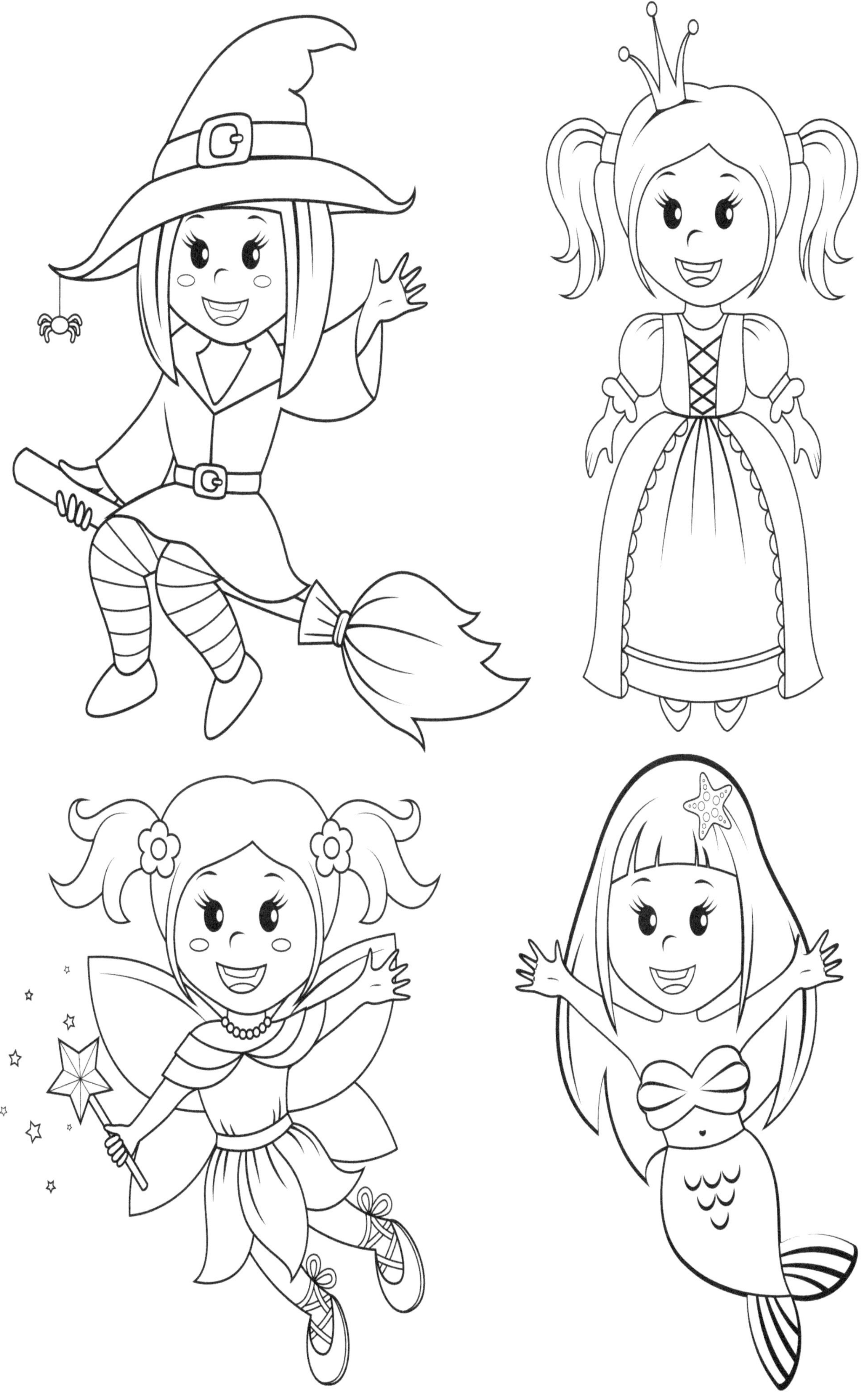

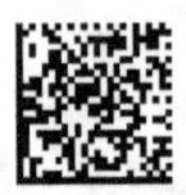

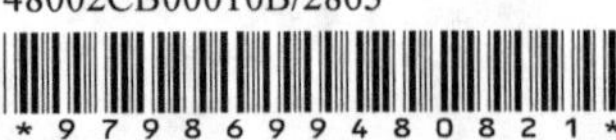